"What is a farm but a mute gospel?
The chaff and the wheat, weeds and plants, blight, rain, insects, sun—
it is a sacred emblem from the first furrow of spring to the last stack
which the snow of winter overtakes in the fields."

RALPH WALDO EMERSON

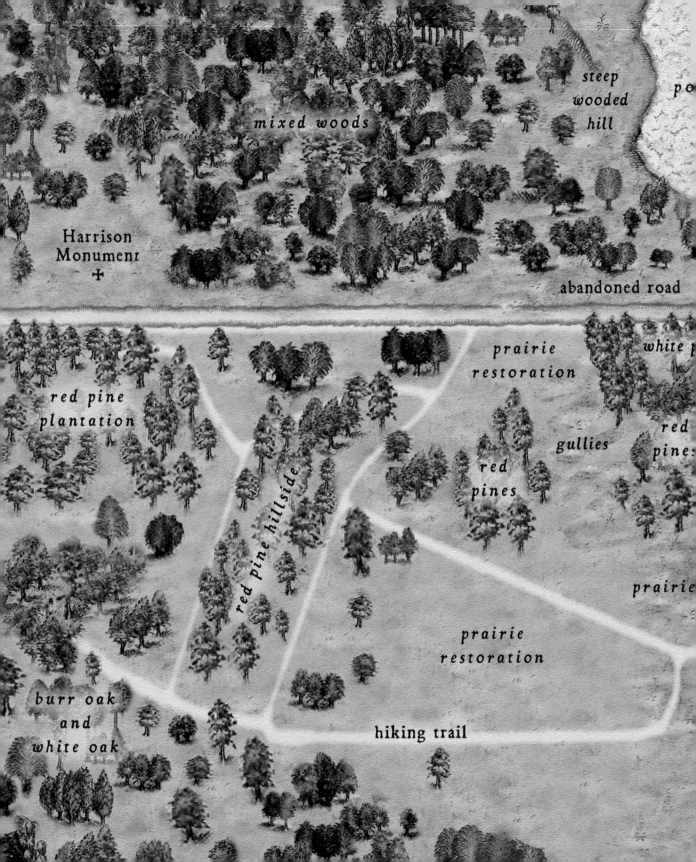

open
field

open
field

black willow windbreak

cabin

garden

pump
house

TOWN ROAD

**wooded
hillside**

apple
tree

site for
first
cabin

black locust hillside

red pines

hiking trail

open field

*white
pine
windbreak*

white pine stand

white pines

hiking trail

lupines

prairie

lupines

Old Farm

A History

JERRY APPS

WITH PHOTOGRAPHS BY STEVE APPS

Wisconsin Historical Society Press

Published by the Wisconsin Historical Society Press
Publishers since 1855

© 2008 by the State Historical Society of Wisconsin
Paperback Edition 2013

For permission to reuse material from *Old Farm: A History* (ISBN 978-0-87020-503-3), please access www.copyright.com or contact the Copyright Clearance Center, Inc. (CCC), 222 Rosewood Drive, Danvers, MA 01923, 978-750-8400. CCC is a not-for-profit organization that provides licenses and registration for a variety of users.

Photographs identified with WHi or WHS are from the Society's collections; address requests to reproduce these photos to the Visual Materials Archivist at Wisconsin Historical Society, 816 State Street, Madison, WI 53706.

wisconsin**history**.org

All photographs by Steve Apps unless otherwise credited.
Photographs on opening pages: page i, the prairie turns golden in fall; page ii, Map by David Michael Miller; page iv, big bluestem

Printed in the United States of America

Designed by Steve Biel

17 16 15 14   5 4 3 2

The Library of Congress has cataloged the hardcover edition as follows:

Apps, Jerold W., 1934–
    Old farm : a history / Jerry Apps ; with photographs by Steve Apps.
      p. cm.
    Includes bibliographical references and index.
     ISBN 978-0-87020-406-7 (hardcover : alk. paper) 1. Waushara County (Wis.)—History, Local.
2. Farm life—Wisconsin—Waushara County. 3. Apps, Jerold W., 1934—Homes and haunts—Wisconsin—Waushara County.
4. Waushara County (Wis.)—Biography. I. Apps, Steve. II. Title.
    F587.W35A77 2008
    977.5'5704—dc22
                              2008004316

∞ The paper used in this publication meets the minimum requirements of the American National Standard for Information Sciences—Permanence of Paper for Printed Library Materials, ANSI Z39.48-1992.

For Josh, Ben, Christian, Nicholas, and Elizabeth,
my grandchildren

Contents

PART I
Beginnings

PART II
Roshara

Prairie grass in spring. Some of our grasses grow three or more feet tall.

Acknowledgments

In 1967 I began writing a weekly column, "Outdoor Notebook," for the *Waushara Argus*. Publisher Howard Sanstadt, now deceased, suggested I include stories about my newly acquired farm. Howard both encouraged and instructed me over a period of ten years while I wrote 520 columns about happenings at my Waushara County property.

Professor Robert Gard, folklorist and writing instructor with the University of Wisconsin Extension, read several of my newspaper columns and suggested I write a book about my family's farm adventures. He helped me through the many challenges of book writing and became my writing mentor. To him I am ever grateful. *The Land Still Lives* was published by Wisconsin House in 1970. Brief excerpts appear in *Old Farm*.

Jim Christensen, Wisconsin Department of Natural Resources (DNR), became interested in our prairie restoration and our Karner blue butterfly population. He provided me with reference material, invited me to a Midwest conference on prairie restoration, and introduced me to Dave Lentz, also with the Wisconsin DNR. Dave is an expert on Karner blue butterflies, a nationally endangered species that needs lupines for its survival. Dave helped us first identify our Karner blues—we have several little blue butterflies that flit around our farm that are not Karner blues. He also read some of the manuscript and made important corrections.

Karner blue butterfly

Neil Dibold, Prairie Nursery, Westfield, Wisconsin, was of enormous help with the identification of wildflowers, grasses, and trees at our farm. I especially appreciate his help in not only correctly identifying the plants but providing accurate Latin names. My brother Darrel, a horticulture PhD, owns and operates a plant nursery in New Jersey. He was once part owner of my farm and helped me with plant identification and Latin names. My brother Donald, who owns thirty-five acres of the original farm and lives on the place, has been a constant source of information as we together recalled the years when we planted several thousand trees.

Pam Anderson, president of the Wild Rose Historical Society, helped me sort out Tom Stewart's Civil War military history. Several men named Tom Stewart fought in the Civil War, and I couldn't figure out which was the first owner of our farm. Pam pointed me in the right direction. Dorothy Luening, a volunteer with the Wisconsin Historical Society, helped me prepare a National Archives application to obtain detailed information about the correct Tom Stewart.

Marvin Wagner, then mayor of Wautoma, Wisconsin, and an active member of the Waushara County Historical Society, encouraged me in my historical diggings and gave me valuable information about Waushara County history.

Linda Steffen, head librarian at Patterson Memorial Library in Wild Rose, directed me toward the collection of *Wild Rose Times* newspapers, along with historical minutes of the Wild Rose village board that are shelved in the library. I used this material extensively.

Rob Nurre, Wisconsin Commissioner of Public Lands Office, was a font of information about early Wisconsin land surveys. He also helped me sort out the history of the Harrison monument used to mark survey section corners (I have one on my farm).

My son Steve, a photographer for the *Wisconsin State Journal*, took all the contemporary photos in the book. He also read and commented on the manuscript from its early development. My son Jeff, a businessman in Colorado, offers broad perspectives and gives me many useful comments on my various book projects, this one included. My daughter, Sue, an elementary teacher in Madison, has a keen editorial eye. She finds many errors that I miss, and she is always asking, "What is this? What does this mean?" It's helpful to have representatives from another generation ask questions about what I too often believe everyone knows.

My wife, Ruth, as she has for more than thirty-five years, reads every book manuscript, usually several times. I listen carefully to her suggestions for improving my writing and continue to thank her.

Kate Thompson, my Wisconsin Historical Society Press editor, constantly amazes me with her ability to take my sometimes poorly organized work and turn it into something much better than I thought possible. I can't thank her enough.

Introduction

This is a story of an old farm, a scant sixty-five acres in Waushara County, Wisconsin, about ninety miles north of Madison and forty-five miles west of Oshkosh. It is located in the Town of Rose, which was named by settlers who moved here from Rose, New York, in the mid-1800s.

The story is about the great glacier that slowly progressed from what is now Canada, digging out the valleys, forming the hills, and leaving behind stones of every shape and size when the ice retreated. It is about the Native Americans who lived on these acres for hundreds of years, tapping the maple trees, trapping the beaver and muskrat, and fishing the streams and lakes long before the first white explorers arrived.

The story is about the first settlers who tilled these hilly, sandy acres after breaking the ground with oxen and heavy-beamed breaking plows, turning under native grasses that sometimes grew taller than the ox teams.

And it is about the years that my family has owned these acres, from 1964 to the present. We've cared for this farm not so much to make a living as to enhance our lives.

From land that provided only a marginal living for its early owners, this place we call Roshara has provided much for my family and me. Each year we harvest the bounty of our garden; gather wild grapes, plums, and cherries for jelly; and cut a few trees for firewood to heat our cabin. We have undertaken one major logging operation to thin pine plantations and remove undesirable tree species. I have hunted deer here for more than four decades; more recently, I've hunted here with my brothers, sons, and nephews for turkeys, ducks, and grouse.

A grasshopper explores a daylily flower.

But far more significant than the material gifts are the spiritual ones we harvest from our farm during all the seasons of the year. More than anything, these sandy acres, some wooded, some prairie, and some wetland, have enhanced our lives and given us new, richer perspectives about the land and all that it comprises.

As we have taken from this farm and at the same time labored to preserve and protect it, we have struggled with age-old questions about people's relationship to the land. The natural world is a vast expanse of overlapping layers of facts, ideas, and perspectives, understandable at one level and incomprehensible at another. It is always the same, yet always changing. It is science and mystery, chaos and calm. Its value exceeds by many times the sum of its parts.

Botanists and zoologists, ecologists and environmentalists have long sought to label, categorize, research, and understand the elements of nature. But they are deluded in thinking that they understand, that they *know*, once they have labeled and categorized. Such work is only a feeble beginning in comprehending the natural world and its intricate relationships.

Likewise, much of our learning about the land is draped in technical matters: classification, scientific study, and cause-and-effect relationships. What is often missing is what Aldo Leopold called a land ethic. Story and history. Community and compassion. The bigger picture.

To value the land and the natural world demands an appreciation that goes deeper than knowing, deeper even than understanding—to the level that involves not only the head, but also the heart.

Built by John Coombes nearly one hundred years ago, the pump house is one of the original farm buildings.

PART I

Beginnings

Rabbit-foot clover

Chapter 1

◇◇◇◇◇◇◇◇◇◇◇◇◇◇◇◇◇◇◇◇◇

Our Farm

*"One swallow does not make a summer, but one skein of geese,
cleaving the murk of a March thaw, is the spring."*
ALDO LEOPOLD

I grew up with my brothers, twins Donald and Darrel, on a 160-acre farm in Waushara County, Wisconsin. My parents, Herman and Eleanor Apps, farmed through the Depression years of the 1930s, the war years of the early 1940s, and the postwar years when farming changed dramatically—tractors replaced horses, electricity replaced lamps and lanterns, milking machines took over from hand milking, grain combines made threshing crews obsolete, indoor plumbing became available, and television eliminated much neighborhood visiting.

After my brothers and I left the home farm in the 1950s, Dad continued farming by himself, caring for a small herd of Holstein cattle and raising enough crops to support the cows. In 1964 Dad sold his cows at auction, and we knew he would eventually sell the farm as well. We all understood that walking the fields of the home place would soon come to an end.

By the mid-1960s I was married and had three small children. We lived in Madison, where I taught agricultural education courses at the University of Wisconsin and Ruth taught part time at Madison Area Technical College, but we continued visiting the home farm regularly. I wanted my children, two sons and a daughter, to experience some of what I had experienced as a child, to gain the appreciation for the land that I had acquired by growing up on a farm. I longed to buy some land of my own, but supporting a family on teachers' salaries left no money for purchasing a place in the country.

The mid-1960s were difficult years in this country. After the Gulf of Tonkin Resolution on August 7, 1964, the United States began sending large numbers of troops to Vietnam. By the end of 1965 troop levels had increased to 125,000 and B-52 bombers began their bombing runs. Sit-ins and student protests against U.S. involvement sprung up on college campuses around the nation, starting at the University of Michigan at Ann Arbor on March 24, 1965. The University of Wisconsin's Madison campus became a center of protest, with sit-ins, police-student confrontations, confusion, demonstrations, and tear gas hanging heavy in the night air. Sirens blared; bullhorns blasted for attention.

The contrast between the UW–Madison campus and life in Waushara County at that time was nearly unfathomable. The home farm was a peaceful place. But as they tended their crops and milked their cows, farmers were well aware that several thousand miles away a war raged. Several local boys had been drafted. Newspaper headlines shouted about battles and deaths.

But the war and the protests weren't the only reason for my interest in returning to the country. As a boy growing up in rural Wisconsin, I had developed an abiding interest in forestry, wildflowers, wildlife, and the outdoors. One of my favorite 4-H Club projects was forestry: during the mid-1940s I planted a few hundred trees each year on the home farm and kept a careful record of their survival and growth rates. By the mid-1960s many of these trees were twenty feet tall.

Knowing my interest in nature and the out-of-doors, my high school speech teacher, Paul Wright, encouraged me to write an original oration for the state high school forensics competition. My speech, "The Hole in Uncle Sam's Pocket," called for soil conservation. I received a runner-up award at a regional speaking contest in Stevens Point.

In 1959, when I worked for the University of Wisconsin as a 4-H youth agent, I read Aldo Leopold's now-famous book *A Sand County Almanac*, published the year after Leopold's death in 1948. I discovered a copy while supervising a group at a 4-H conservation camp. I was amazed at Leopold's writing skills and his ability to talk about the land and its preservation in fresh ways.

From Leopold I learned that a relationship with the land involves much more than hiking and identifying, more than wood chopping and tree planting. I learned that a true connection to the land requires thinking, feeling, and acting that comes from deep within and that can be cultivated and nurtured throughout a lifetime.

Soon I was reading about another Wisconsin boy, John Muir, born in Scotland in 1838 but raised here in Marquette County. Muir has rightfully been called the father of our national park system. His wonderful little book *The Story of My Boyhood and Youth* set the stage for his career devoted to the study of nature and the protection of the environment. Muir taught me the power of wonder, of searching and exploring, of looking and, more important, learning how to see. He helped me recognize the importance of leaving something of value for the next generation—a little piece of the outdoors to enjoy and appreciate.

I first learned about Henry David Thoreau in high school but at the time had little love for his writing. As I grew older I appreciated his words more and more. Thoreau's writing has taken me some work to decipher, but its philosophical perspective and deep insights into the natural world continue to impress me. In *Walden*, he wrote, "I found in myself, and still find, an instinct toward a higher, or, as it is named, spiritual life, as do most men, and another toward a primitive rank and savage one, and I reverence them both. I love the wild not less than the good." Those words require some pondering, but that's what I like about his work. Every time I read Thoreau, I discover new meanings and ideas. And I admire Thoreau's simple lifestyle, his craving for solitude, and his vast curiosity about all things in the natural world.

My high school English teacher, Miss Arlene Holt, introduced me to Ralph Waldo Emerson, but not until maybe twenty years ago did I discover his powerful book *Nature*. There I encountered the stunning, "Nothing in nature is exhausted in its first use. When a thing has served an end to the uttermost, it is wholly new for an ulterior service . . . every end is converted into a new means." Emerson helped me see the more profound effects of a relationship to the land—of the spiritual dimensions and the poetic qualities. Of the behind-the-scenes power of being in connection with the land.

Sigurd Olson grew up in northern Wisconsin and is probably best known for helping to protect the Boundary Waters Canoe Area Wilderness in northern Minnesota. For each of twenty-five years I have spent a week in late summer with one or more family members canoeing in the Boundary Waters. Reading Olson's *Listening Point*, my favorite of his books, I am reminded of my adventures there. Olson wrote, "Campsites in the north are chosen for the things you can see at a distance, a landing for the canoe and outfit and place for the tent. But they are loved and remembered for the things you cannot see." Like Thoreau, Olson grasped the importance of a escaping to a sacred place, to a cabin in the woods or on a lake, a place away from the sounds and fury of everyday life, a place for contemplation and discovery.

In summer our pond
attracts all manner of
creatures.

Rachel Carson's *Silent Spring* awakened many to the powerful aftereffects of pesticides such as DDT. I was working for the UW Extension in Green Bay when *Silent Spring* hit the best-seller lists in the early 1960s. I was impressed with Carson's research and her vision, but I was in awe that a scientist could write in an understandable, even lyrical way. She wrote, "The history of life on earth has been a history of interaction between living things and their surroundings." Such common sense, yet so often ignored.

Of course, I knew of Gaylord Nelson as a Wisconsin senator (1949–1959) and governor (1959–1963) and admired his work in preserving the environment. I met him when he wrote an introduction to my first book, *The Land Still Lives*, published in 1970, and I followed his career and work closely. Nelson also served in the U.S. Senate from 1963 to 1981. During one of his first Senate speeches, in 1963, he said, "We need a comprehensive and nationwide program to save the national resources of America. We cannot be blind to the growing crisis of our environment. Our soil, our water, and our air are becoming more polluted every day. Our most priceless natural resources—trees, lakes, rivers, wildlife habitats, scenic landscapes—are being destroyed."

Nelson turned the attention of thousands, maybe millions, toward the importance of preserving the environment. He is perhaps best known as the founder of Earth Day, April 22. At a rally I attended during Earth Week in spring of 1970, more than two thousand University of Wisconsin students gave Senator Nelson a standing ovation at the beginning and end of his talk—a rare thing for university students to do in those days. At the rally Nelson said, "Our goal is an environment of decency, equality, and mutual respect for all other human beings and all other creatures. An environment without ugliness, without ghettos, without discrimination, without hunger, without poverty, and without war."

All of these influences—dreams of escaping the turmoil of the city and introducing my children to a lifestyle I'd grown up with, an awareness that my parents would soon move to town, my lifelong interest in nature and the environment—helped make clear in a simple but compelling way the desire for a piece of land to call my own.

Then one day in the fall of 1964, while he was at the courthouse in Wautoma, my dad learned that the Coombes place was for sale, an abandoned farm no more than two miles south of our home place. The land had been abandoned after a disastrous fire in 1959 and had come up for sale when Mrs. Coombes died earlier in 1964 at the age of eighty-eight. One weekend when I was home, Dad asked me what I thought about him buying the place. The price, he said, essentially covered the back taxes owed.

I was elated. The Coombes farm was smaller than the home place, only a hundred acres, but in some ways it was more interesting because it included a five-acre pond. Although our home farm boasted twenty acres of woods, it was on high ground with no stream or pond.

When I was a boy, it was customary on Sunday afternoons to walk not only on our land but on the neighbors' as well. In those days there weren't any No Trespassing signs; we could walk almost anywhere, and we did. I remembered walking to the Coombes place with Dad one fall day. As we approached the pond, wild ducks lifted from the water—a huge flock, as I recall. The Coombes farm also had paper birch trees, and black willow, and black locust—we had none of those in our woods two miles away. The home farm was hilly, but not nearly so much so as the Coombes place. That in itself was interesting; you never know what's on the other side of a hill.

My dad knew I wanted land, and my brothers, Darrel and Don, had similar interests. And Dad also wanted a place for himself, a place where he could escape from "all those people" in town, where he knew he and my mother would move in a few years. In those days Wild Rose boasted about six hundred people—a crowd to Dad, who was accustomed to having no neighbors closer than a half mile. Dad wanted a place where he could watch the sun rise and set, unencumbered by buildings, electric lines, or other man-made obstacles. He wanted to look to the horizon and not see another person.

In 1964 Dad bought the Coombes property, as much for himself and my mother as for my brothers and me. In 1966 he sold the property to Darrel, Don, and me for one dollar.

Some forty years later, Roshara has become a touchstone in all our lives, a place where we have both discovered and maintained our connections to the land, a place where my three children and now their children have gained an appreciation for the land that transcends anything conveyed by a textbook, a film, or a video.

In 1966 our three children were of preschool age. In 2006 Susan, who lives in Madison, has two children: Josh, fourteen, and Ben, ten. Steve, who spent several years in Florida, and his partner, Natasha, also live in Madison. Jeff and his wife, Sandy, live in Colorado with their three children: Christian, nine; Nicholas, seven; and Elizabeth, two.

All of them are part of this story.

Prairie grasses and wildflowers in late fall

Chapter 2

◇◇◇◇◇◇◇◇◇◇◇◇◇◇◇◇◇◇◇◇

Skunk's Hollow

"Can't grow much more than sand burs. Tough place to make a living."
HERMAN APPS

After Dad had purchased the Coombes farm, I remembered that the community where the farm was located had the less-than-auspicious name "Skunk's Hollow." When I asked Dad how the area got its name, he shrugged as if to say it should be obvious. (I suspect that with the several small ponds in the area, there may have been more skunks than usual.)

When I was five or six years old, Dad drove me to a farm near ours that had once been owned by my Grandpa Apps. This 160-acre farm, already abandoned by the late 1930s, was about a mile southwest of the Coombes farm. Rambling along in our 1930s Willys car, we passed through Skunk's Hollow. We crossed hard-surfaced County Highway A and drove past the Chain O' Lake School, with its red woodshed and outhouses, one in each corner of the school lot. The sandy road twisted around Chain O' Lake and then climbed again, passing the Coombes place on the right and the Floyd Jeffers farm on the left. "Poor farms," Dad said. "Sandy farms—can't grow much more than sand burs. Tough place to make a living."

These were Depression years, and it was difficult for anyone to make a living no matter where they lived or how good their farms. Those who lived on the poorer farms especially suffered.

"Farm folks with little money live off their vegetable gardens," Dad told me. "They've got milk and butter from their cows, and they usually butcher a hog in the fall. They don't go hungry. Biggest problem they got is paying their taxes every year, and if they got a mortgage on their farm, then they really got a problem." I surely didn't understand everything my dad was telling me, but I could tell who lived poor just by looking: buildings without paint, skinny livestock, worn-out farm implements rusting in the yard.

On top of a rise beyond the Jeffers farm, we turned on a road leading west and dropped down to go around Wagner's Lake and Wagner's farm, then climbed to the top of another hill where Dad stopped the car next to a clump of huge cottonwood trees.

"This is Grandpa's old farm," Dad said. The barn had disappeared, but the old house, long abandoned, stood tucked against an oak woodlot that led to a pond a short hike down the hill.

The house had never been painted, but there was a certain beauty to the old gray boards, cracked and curled from years of blistering summer heat and frigid winters. The windows were broken, and the kitchen door hung by one hinge. A huge lilac bush stood to one side of the back door, and a box elder tree had grown through the broken boards of the front porch.

For a long time we stood looking at this weathered old house and listening to the breeze rustling the cottonwood leaves and inhaling the smells of summer. I wondered why we were standing there, doing nothing, but I stood quietly next to Dad, holding his hand and wondering what he was seeing that I couldn't see. I learned a valuable lesson that day. When two people look at the same thing, they often see something quite different.

When I was older I knew what Dad saw that day. He saw his mother and father, his brothers, Fred, Ed, George, and John, and his sisters, Doris, Irene, Elsie, and Minnie. It looked like an old house to me, a forgotten farm with trees growing where cattle once grazed. But to Dad it was much more. It was a place with meaning, a place with memories.

Dad pushed aside the kitchen door, and we walked among the clutter of broken glass, fallen plaster, and scraps of wallpaper hanging loose from the walls. In what had been the kitchen, he showed me where the cookstove had once stood, where the stovepipe went into the chimney, where the kitchen table had been, where his mother and sisters had washed dishes, where they kept the pail for drinking water. As we walked through the dining room he pointed out the stairway to the upstairs where he and his brothers and sisters had slept.

Back outside again he told me stories about hunting squirrels and rabbits, and Canada geese and mallards when they came down from the north each fall. He told me about hoeing corn and making hay, about milking cows and walking to country school. About digging potatoes and raising rutabagas. For him, this old, abandoned farm was more than an unpainted house with a leaky roof and a tree growing through the front porch. It was more than tree-studded acres that once grew potatoes and corn, oats and rye and provided pasture land for a few broken-down milk cows. This old farm was part of who he was. It shaped his life in ways that he wasn't fully aware of. Yet he knew something of the power of this land, and he wanted me to experience it, too.

I didn't just become aware of Skunk's Hollow that day, a little of its history and mystique, a little about people once there and still there. That day I began to learn something about how a piece of land can shape a person—influence how he thinks and what he believes.

Looking back, that early memory of Skunk's Hollow and the visit to my grandfather's old farm made my father's purchase of the Coombes place even more compelling. In a way I was coming home, destined to learn some of what my grandfather and father had learned working these hilly acres.

Field road on the way to the prairie

Chapter 3

Terminal Moraine and Tension Zone

"The soil is generally not suited to corn or other row crops because of the high susceptibility to soil blowing and water erosion."

1985 SOIL SURVEY

Every piece of land has a story to tell: of buildings and fences, of crops and woodlots and weather, and of course of the people who lived on it. One of the earliest, most dramatic events that shaped our Skunk's Hollow farm was the last glacier. This huge sheet of ice began moving into what is now Wisconsin some twenty-five thousand years ago, pushing over the land, tearing, ripping, and burying everything in its path.[1] The great glacier that formed the state's topography had six lobes, all of which extended south but missed southwestern Wisconsin. The Green Bay Lobe formed our farm, created the hills and valleys, and in its retreat ten thousand years ago left behind stones of many sizes, shapes, and colors, from pebbles to some as big as automobiles.

The glacier also left behind a string of ponds: Wagner's Lake, then our pond, then an unnamed one to the north of us, and then the largest, named Chain O' Lake. These small lakes and ponds formed when huge chunks of buried ice melted, leaving water-filled depressions. None of these ponds has an inlet or outlet, but each is fed by springs and natural runoff.

Our land is part of a moraine, or ridge of glacial deposit, that extends north to Stevens Point and south to Rock County. The moraine marks the site where the glacier stopped its southward progression and began retreating. Just to the west of our place is the Glacial Lake Wisconsin Basin, a huge area that was once covered with meltwater from the many years' accumulation of ice. Today it is a vast, sandy, irrigated vegetable-growing area—flat as the surface of the lake it once was, compared to the hills and valleys of our farm. It is a massive source of water just a few feet below the surface. Eventually, as the ice continued to melt and Glacial Lake Wisconsin grew larger, a wall of water forced its way south, forming the Wisconsin Dells. The Wisconsin River, which flows about twenty-five miles west of our farm through this once lake, now flat land, is a reminder of the glacier's work.

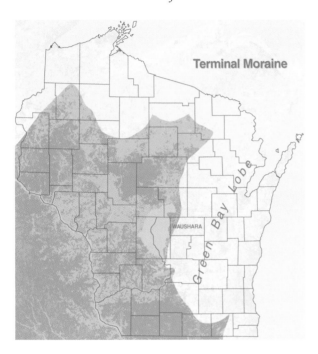

UW–MADISON, DEPT. OF GEOGRAPHY, CARTOGRAPHY LAB

The Ice Age Trail, one of only eight National Scenic Trails in the United States, passes a short distance from the western edge of our property, providing a place for hikers and explorers to see firsthand evidence of the glacier's massive force and what it left behind.

Running north-south through the terminal moraine is a divide that splits the direction of the groundwater here as well as the direction of nearby streams and rivers. Two miles west of our farm, on the west side of the divide, water flows west to the Wisconsin River and then on to the Mississippi River and the Gulf of Mexico. At our farm, the rivers and streams flow east, eventually into Green Bay and on to the Atlantic Ocean. A landowner's well two miles west of our farm reaches water at twenty feet, and our well is sixty feet deep. But a neighbor living directly on the divide has to go more than two hundred feet to get water for his well.

Floyd Jeffers, who lived across the road from our farm all his life, once told me that we had the best water in Waushara County. There was truth to his statement; we tap into the aquifer at its beginning, before the water has an opportunity to pick up contaminants.

In 1913 the Wisconsin Geological and Natural History Survey published the results of a soil survey of Waushara County. The lead author wrote, "[Waushara County] is made up of numerous hills, pothole depressions and narrow, irregular ridges and valleys. The hills vary in height from 30 to 100 feet or more above the Wisconsin River Valley."[2]

According to the survey, our farm's topsoil consisted of light brown sand of medium texture with little organic material and low water-holding capacity. The real meaning of this: We've got poor soil that requires lots of rain before crops amount to anything.

More than seventy years later, the National Cooperative Soil Survey (College of Agriculture and Life Sciences, UW–Madison, and Soil Conservation Service) conducted its own soil survey of Waushara County in 1985–1986.[3] By this time the soil scientists had come up with new, more sophisticated ways to describe the poor soil in our area.

Art Peterson, longtime soil science professor at UW–Madison and a neighbor in Madison, prepared an updated soil survey for our farm in 2004. Art said we had five types of soil: Richford loamy sand (6–12 percent slope), Richford loamy sand (12–20 percent slope), Coloma loamy sand (6–12 percent slope), Okee loamy sand (12–20 percent slope), and Okee loamy sand (2–6 percent slope). The higher the percentage of slope, the hillier the land. Most of our farm falls within the Okee loamy sand category. Soil scientists in 1985 described it this way: "Surface area is a dark brown loamy sand about two inches thick. Subsoil extends to a depth of about sixty-inches. . . . Most areas are used as woodland. A few are used as cropland or pasture."[4]

Soil scientists classed some of our acres as Coloma loamy sand, describing it this way: "This sloping, excessively drained soil is on the sides of ridges and knolls on moraines. The soil is generally not suited to corn or other row crops because of the high susceptibility to soil blowing and water erosion."[5]

Knee-high sweet corn in the garden—and it's still June.

Over the years I have found one area on the farm where the soil is somewhat heavier than elsewhere, containing more organic material and with a stickier subsoil. The soil in this two-acre field doesn't fit any of the scientists' categories, as the soil contains a goodly amount of clay. Here's how I know. A few years ago, in April, I was plowing the small field near a white pine windbreak a couple hundred yards south of my cabin. The frost wasn't entirely out of the ground, especially on the north side of the windbreak, where my tractor became impossibly

Pine and black locust

stuck on a little knoll, sinking through the topsoil into the stickiest of sticky soils my tractor and I had ever encountered. It took me more than two hours to ease my little John Deere out of the sticky subsoil that sucked at my tractor's tires like quicksand.

Both the early and the more recent soil surveyors documented the crops growing in the area. Potatoes were the main crop in 1913, yielding 75 to 125 bushels per acre, up to 250 bushels per acre in a wet year and grown on the heavier soils. Other major crops were corn (20 to 35 bushels per acre), rye (10 bushels per acre), and navy beans (no yields reported).[6]

Where potatoes are grown today in the Town of Rose and in the townships to the west, yields were about 800 bushels per acre in 2004. Corn yields in 2004 and 2005 averaged about 130 bushels per acre.[7] The soil here hasn't changed, but agricultural practices have. Most of today's high yields result from irrigation and ample amounts of fertilizer.

Without irrigation, the relatively recent 1985 soil survey scientists said my predominantly Okee loamy sand soil should yield seventy bushels of corn per acre, sixty-five bushels of oats, three and a half tons of bromegrass alfalfa hay, or twenty-four bushels of soybeans. Of course, these yields assume a growing season of average rainfall. Because these sandy soils dry out so quickly, unless rain comes regularly throughout the growing season, yields are severely reduced, some years providing no crop at all.

The soil surveyors in 1985 recommended tree species for my Okee loamy sand. Hardwoods: northern pin oak and black oak. Coniferous: red pine, jack pine, and eastern white pine. All these tree species and more now grow on my farm. We have planted only the red pine; the rest have grown naturally.

~~~~~~

Sometimes I hear visitors to our state claim that they pass through a "tension zone" when they drive through central Wisconsin and on into the state's northern vacationlands. They are usually referring to their mental state. But my farm rests near the middle of a true biological tension zone as well.[8]

This tension zone, defined by biologists, is an imaginary band twenty or thirty miles wide that passes through northwestern Wisconsin, then through the central part of the state, and on south, ending at Lake Michigan south of Sheboygan. Within this band, plant and animal species from northern and southern Wisconsin overlap. Bur oak grows in southern Wisconsin but not in the northern part of the state. White pine grows naturally in the north but not in the south. Black bear roam the north but not the south (although it appears bears are moving farther south each year due to loss of habitat). Yet we have bur oak, white pine, and black bears at our farm.

Amazingly, our farm is on the intersection of the terminal moraine and the biological tension zone. I tell my grandsons that because

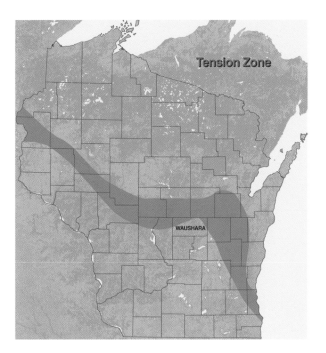

UW–MADISON, DEPT. OF GEOGRAPHY, CARTOGRAPHY LAB

of this unusual coming together, our farm is a place where strange creatures can be found. We might discover exotic plants and animals and even buried gems transported from northern Canada. "Sure, Grandpa," the boys say.

But there is some truth behind the claims. Diamonds have been found in glacial leavings near Eagle in Waukesha County, southwest of Oregon in Dane County, and in Ozaukee, Racine, and Washington Counties. The largest weighed more than fifteen carats. As long ago as 1670 Jesuit fathers told stories of diamonds found on several islands at the entrance to Green Bay.[9]

Aside from the skepticism about tension zones and terminal moraines, land at this intersection does provide interesting perspectives beyond the tall tales.

Chapter 4

◇◇◇◇◇◇◇◇◇◇◇◇◇◇◇◇◇◇◇

Surveys, Maps, and First People

"This Township is mostly made up of a high ridge of barren hills on which there is very little timber, but which are covered with a stunted growth of black oak brush."

SURVEYOR Ira Cook

The view west from the prairie

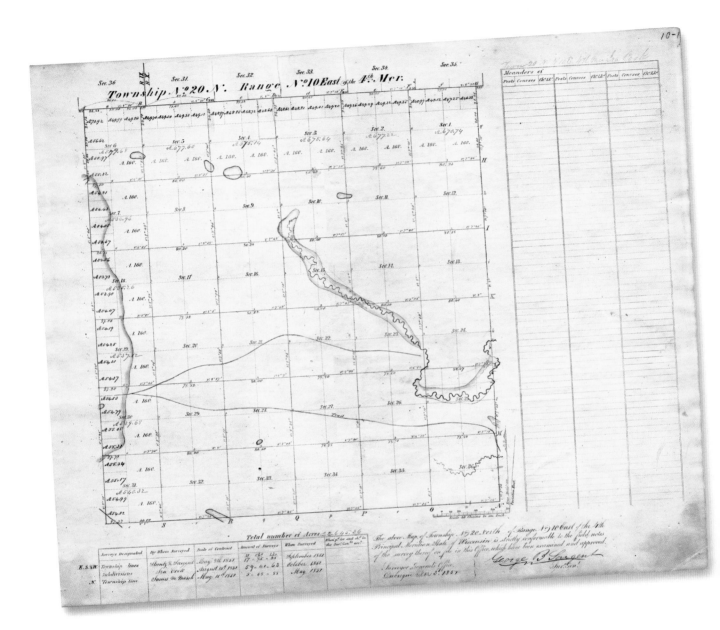

May 1851 survey map for the Town of Rose, showing section numbers

COURTESY OF THE WISCONSIN BOARD OF COMMISSIONERS OF PUBLIC LANDS

Long before soil scientists declared my land marginal for farming, federal government surveyors said the same thing. G. R. Stuntz and J. O. Sargent worked their way across northern Waushara County in May 1851, conducting what was called an "exterior survey," which divided the county into townships.[1] With their survey team, which consisted of two chainmen (John Sinclair and Elisha Whitney) and two axmen (John Chisholm and Chester Coburn), they divided the county into eighteen townships and established the official township dividing lines. In their survey notes about what was to become Rose Township, Stuntz and Sargent wrote, "Surface rolling, soil sandy, second rate. No timber. Oak brush, willow and grass."[2] Not a glowing report.

On October 2, 1851, Ira Cook and his survey crew began an "interior survey" of the township that later became known as Rose.[3] Cook and his crew, consisting of assistant surveyor John Rogan, four chainmen (J. B. Salisbury, J. B. Potter, C. B. McLaughlin, and Daniel Gallager), and two axmen (S. Wright and George Wier), established section (640 acres) and quarter-section (160 acres) boundaries within the townships.

Imagine what it must have been like for a survey crew to enter what was still wild country. They had no nearby town for provisions, no roof over their heads on rainy nights except a canvas tent. They camped their way through the countryside, measuring and making maps and writing notes about what they saw. Not many miles to the south, farmers grew wheat by the hundreds of acres, but in this new territory there was nothing but sandy, rock-strewn hills, some open prairie, and black oaks and white oaks.

Like Stuntz and Sargent, Ira Cook didn't think much of the land that is now our farm. Nor did he have much positive to say about the township where the farm is located. He wrote, "This Township is mostly made up of a high ridge of barren hills on which there is very little

A page from Ira Cook's survey notes describing our land, 1851

COURTESY OF THE WISCONSIN BOARD OF COMMISSIONERS OF PUBLIC LANDS

timber, but which are covered with a stunted growth of black oak brush. There is very little arable land in the township. . . . The eastern part of the township, however [words not legible] and contains some good soil. Where the land is at all adapted to cultivation, the soil is first rate. . . . [There] are several small lakes and ponds, and one small creek [now known as the Upper Pine River] that rises in Section 10 and runs in a southeast course through the township."[4] Cook also noted that the hills here were filled with "granite boulders."

These survey crews may have been the first nonnative visitors to much of Rose Township. That October of 1851 Cook wrote in his leather-bound log book, ". . . the township . . . as yet contains no settlers."[5] Of course, native people had spent thousands of years on these lands, trapping, tapping maple trees, and hunting.

The government survey that divided most of the United States into townships, sections, and quarter sections resulted from the Federal Land Ordinances of 1784, 1785, and 1787 and the Land Act of 1796. The survey excluded the original thirteen states, Vermont, Texas, Hawaii, parts of southern California, and parts of Maine. Many of those states used the British metes and bounds system, which described property lines based on what the eye could see—and often included in property descriptions such landmarks as trees, rivers, and other physical features that could and did change over time.

The U.S. government survey of which our farm is a part began in 1785 at the Pennsylvania border with Ohio and proceeded westward. Native American tribes occupied most of these lands at the time, so before the federal government could survey and sell the lands it "negotiated" treaties with the tribes. In most cases the government forced these treaties upon the Indians, creating untold strife and unhappiness among the native peoples who had lived on these lands for centuries.

At the heart of this tragic conflict was differing approaches to the land. Owning land was a European-American idea, at odds with Native American philosophies of sharing vast areas of land. Before whites arrived, the idea of individuals owning a piece of ground was largely eschewed by these early peoples who lived on what is now our farm.

In Wisconsin, much of the land west of Lake Poygan, north of the Fox River, and east of the Wisconsin River had been Menominee Indian territory until 1848. In that year, the year Wisconsin became a state, the Menominee ceded the last of their land to the United States in the Treaty of Lake Poygan (Lake Pow-aw-hay-kon-nay), signed on October 18. The treaty, ratified January 23, 1849, promised the Menominee a new homeland of 600,000 acres in

Minnesota, plus $350,000—$150,000 for moving expenses and the remaining $200,000 to be paid in equal cash installments over ten years beginning in 1857. The Menominee could continue to live in Wisconsin until 1850.[6] In 1847 the Menominee tribe included about twenty-five hundred people. Of that number it is estimated that twenty-two hundred lived by hunting and fishing and three hundred were farmers. Most of those farming lived near Lake Poygan.[7]

Shortly after the treaty was negotiated in 1848, Chief Oshkosh and several other Menominee chiefs visited the new land in Minnesota; they liked neither the close proximity to the Crow Wing tribe nor the quality of the land. When the representatives returned in 1849, they immediately sent a delegation from the tribe to Washington. Chief Oshkosh made an impassioned speech to President Millard Fillmore, arguing the Menominees' displeasure with the 1848 treaty. According to a translation of his speech, Chief Oshkosh "preferred . . . a home somewhere in Wisconsin, for the poorest region of Wisconsin was better than that of the Crow Wing."[8] In 1852 President Fillmore granted the Menominee a temporary reservation along the Wolf River.

In May 1854 the Menominee, with the consent of the Wisconsin legislature, signed another treaty making the reservation permanent and giving up the promised Minnesota lands. In addition, the federal government would pay the Menominee $242,686 over fifteen years starting in 1857 to cover the difference between the original 600,000 acres they were promised and the 276,480 acres they would now own (and which is now Menomonee County). For all of their millions of acres of Wisconsin lands, the tribe received on average about thirteen cents an acre in payment.[9]

~~~~~~

Wisconsin lands were surveyed between 1833 and 1866. Surveyors established the baseline and meridian in 1832 and then began work in southern Wisconsin, starting at the Wisconsin-Illinois border and a point about ten miles east of the Mississippi River. This Point of Beginnings was the intersection of the state's border with Illinois and the Fourth Principal Meridian. This meridian extends north from the mouth of the Illinois River, between the Grant and Iowa County line, and then through Richland, Vernon, Monroe, Jackson, Clark, Taylor, Price, Ashland, and Iron Counties to Lake Superior.[10]

East-west lines crossing the principal meridian every six miles are township lines. The township numbers reflect how far north a location is from the baseline (the Illinois border) and how far east or west from the Fourth Principal Meridian. Our farm is located twenty townships north of the Illinois border and ten townships east of the Fourth Principal Meridian. Thus the land description of our farm begins: Township 20 North, Range 10 East.

According to standard procedure, surveyor Ira Cook numbered the thirty-six sections, each consisting of 640 acres, starting in the upper right (northeast) corner of the township with number 1 and moving across with section number 36 in the lower right (southeast) corner. Our farm is located in section 33, which is in the bottom row of sections in Rose Township (30 through 36) and near the township boundary line that separates Rose from Wautoma Township to the south.

With the sections properly marked, the survey crew continued to locate quarter sections of 160 acres each, which became a standard farm size for many Midwestern settlers. The complete and official location of our farm in survey language is the "north one half of the southwest one quarter of section 33, township 20 north, range 10 east (80 acres), plus the south twenty (20 acres) of the northwest quarter of section 33, township 20 north, range 10 east, Waushara County, Wisconsin, total acreage, 100." The original parcel was 160 acres, but Tom Stewart, the first owner, sold 60 northern acres in 1877. By knowing the surveyors' land description, I can quickly determine that our farm is twenty townships (20 x 6 miles) or 120 miles from the Illinois border, as the crow flies. Likewise, if we are range 10 east, I know we are 60 miles (10 x 6 miles) from the Fourth Principal Meridian. Straight west of us, the Fourth Meridian passes through Monroe and Jackson Counties.

Surveyor Cook wrote about section 33 and the land that comprises our farm: "Surface hilly. Soil second rate. Timber black, bur and white oak with undergrowth of black oak . . . and hazel brush." In comments about sections 27 and 28, which lie just to the north of our farm, he wrote, "Indian trail bears west."[11] Today County Highway A follows this early Native American route through the area. This county road is now one of the main routes to Wild Rose, the closest village to our farm.

Cook made no mention of meeting Indians as his crew worked across the township, but the Indian trails that he marked on his map continued to be used well into the late 1800s and long after the land was supposedly settled.

With its land survey completed, the U.S. government could now sell the land based on survey descriptions. Land buyers didn't need to step foot on a property to buy it, although most would want to. Even with section 33 surveyed, there were no immediate takers—understandable,

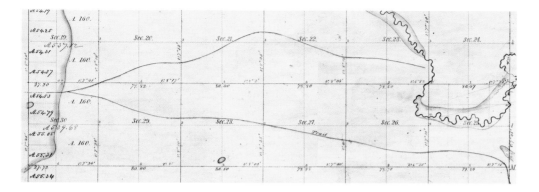

A closeup of the 1851 survey map shows Indian trails crossing Rose Township.
COURTESY OF THE WISCONSIN BOARD OF COMMISSIONERS OF PUBLIC LANDS

because the better land in the township was to the north and east. Checking the Wisconsin Land Patents Database, I learned that Josiah Etheredge and John Etheridge (perhaps relatives, with one name misspelled in the records?) each obtained a land patent in 1855 for eighty acres in sections 25 and 26, just west of present-day Wild Rose. Cornelius Etheridge bought a land patent for forty acres in 1856 and another for forty acres in 1858. Daniel Davies bought eighty acres in section 24 in 1855. Samuel Patterson bought forty acres in section 12 in 1857. That same year, Martin A. Redfield bought forty acres in section 12. Richard Roberts bought forty acres in section 12 in 1857, forty acres in 1858, and another forty in 1861.[12]

But our section 33 sat idle until after the Civil War, which says something about the poor quality of the land, its hills and stony fields. Thomas Stewart acquired what is now my farm in 1867. Milan Jeffers bought a land patent for 160 acres in section 33 in 1873, land directly across the road from my farm. James Jeffers bought the quarter section north of Milan Jeffers in 1874. Remnants of James Jeffers's homestead buildings—stone walls—are still visible.[13]

Who were these early pioneers who ended up on what turned out to be one of the poorest farms in a township of many poor, sandy farms?

Showy goldenrod on the prairie

Chapter 5

°°°°°°°°°°°°°°°°°°°°°°°

Early Settlers

*"Father remarked that wheat was never again as yellow and abundant
as the first harvest they raised."*
JOHN WOODWARD

The earliest recorded story about pioneer settlement on the lands around our farm is a
handwritten autobiography by John M. Woodward, who was born November 11, 1852, on a
farm a mile or so south of our place.[1] Woodward's parents moved from New Hampshire to
central Wisconsin in March 1851. They arrived by boat at Sheboygan and then traveled over
land to Greenbush, Fond du Lac, Berlin (a trading post on the Fox River), and finally Wautoma.
The senior Woodward referred to the area as "Indian land," as indeed it was. John Woodward
was born a year later in a shanty built of rough boards hauled some six miles from a "crude
sawmill" in Wautoma to the land his father had selected. The rustic home was about twelve feet
by twelve feet, with cracks "chinked and battened" to keep out the wet and cold.

John Woodward wrote about his father's recollections of the Indians in the area. "The
Menominee tribe of Indians ranged the country around us, led by Menominee John, a splendid
specimen of savage standing six feet in his moccasins with long black hair and a long nose."[2]

The Woodward family lived in Indian country for but one year before returning to
New Hampshire. Woodward wrote, "It was the isolation, loneliness, and homesickness that
caused them to return east. As far as I can recall from what they said, they made little progress
that first year beyond building their shanty and raising a garden from seeds they brought with
them. For one thing, they raised a great abundance of melons. Such melons as the virgin soil

produced were never raised after the country was settled and the ground used for other purposes. Father remarked that wheat was never again as yellow and abundant as the first harvest they raised."

The Woodward family soon returned to Wisconsin, this time with a second son, who had been born in New Hampshire. Some seventy years later, John Woodward described their lives in the 1850s and 1860s:

The Indians were our nearest neighbors who called most frequently. Deer were seen more than squirrels are now. Venison was the only "beef." I remember in childhood wild meat was the only meat except when pigs were killed in the fall. Bears were often seen, and sometimes killed, but generally not until they had robbed the pig pens. All cattle were saved for cows and oxen. Ox teams were the only ones and only the most fortunate settlers had these.

In the spring passenger pigeons filled the air and often made it as dark as on a cloudy day. Men had to patrol their newly seeded fields with guns every morning and often at other times. I went up and down a field many times keeping pigeons and other wild fowl off.

Prairie hens flew up before us wherever we went. Flocks of wild geese would light and strut over the fields. Millions of game fowl were killed every year, the breast cut out and the rest thrown away. The exceptions were the wild geese and ducks which were fit in their season.

But the poorest people of today [Woodward was writing in the 1920s] know nothing of the poverty of that early time in spite of the abundance of nature. There were no luxuries to be had, if they had the money, and the necessities of today were luxuries then, beyond the reach of all because they were unobtainable.

Only the cheapest grade of cloth was sold in the stores. Many wives of the pioneers spun the flax and wool into yarn after their husbands had broken the flax and carded the wool by hand, and then wove their clothing on primitive looms.

Boots from cowhide were the finest things worn by men. . . . Many mothers bound their children's feet in rags in cold weather.

Cornbread, johnnycake and mush were staple foods together with potatoes and rye bread. Wheat and flour were scarcer and conserved more carefully than during the World War [World War I].

There was pork at killing time for those who were enterprising and thrifty enough to raise pigs and fortunate enough to save them from wild animals. And there was milk and butter when the cows came in (a calf was born and the cow once more gave milk).

The prairie in early fall

Our treat for company was turnips. We would bring up a basket of them. All would sit around and talk and scrape turnips until 12 o'clock or often later. Then before separating they would have a session of prayer and sing the old hymns sung in the east or even in England.[3]

Living conditions challenged the sturdiest of the settlers who lived in Waushara County and the Township of Rose in the late 1850s through the 1860s. These were the conditions that Thomas Stewart, the first pioneer owner of our land, faced when he arrived in 1867.

When Tom Stewart farmed these acres, he made hay by cutting it and then drying it in little piles, sometimes called haycocks.
He hauled the dry hay to his barn, where he stored it for winter feed.

Chapter 6

Tom Stewart

"[A]ny person who is the head of a family, or who has arrived at the age of twenty-one years, and is a citizen of the United States, . . . shall from and after the first of January, eighteen hundred and sixty-three, be entitled to enter one quarter section or a less quantity of unappropriated public lands. . . ."

THE HOMESTEAD ACT, 1862

At the height of the Civil War, on May 20, 1862, the U.S. Congress passed the Homestead Act. President Lincoln signed it into law that same year. The law—whose purpose, of course, was to encourage settlement of land in the west—declared "[t]hat any person who is the head of a family, or who has arrived at the age of twenty-one years, and is a citizen of the United States, or who shall have filed his declaration of intention to become such, as required by the naturalization laws of the United States, and who has never borne arms against the United States Government or given aid and comfort to its enemies, shall from and after the first of January, eighteen hundred and sixty-three, be entitled to enter one quarter section or a less quantity of unappropriated public lands. . . ." Those who met these requirements, who lived on and cultivated their parcel for a minimum of five years, and who paid a small filing fee, were eligible for a quarter section, or 160 acres, at no cost. The act gave priority to Union veterans, who could deduct the number of years served in the war from the five-year residency requirement. (As the language of the law made clear: Confederate soldiers need not apply.)

The land that would become our farm remained in government ownership until 1867, two years after the end of the war. While other farms had begun to spring up in the township of Rose, our land, with its sandy soil and steep hills, remained much as it was when the last great glacier formed it ten thousand years ago. But in 1866 Union veteran Tom Stewart, a

New York native whose family moved to Waushara County sometime before the Civil War, returned to Wisconsin to look for homestead lands. Several of his friends from New York lived in Rose Township, and he soon found an eligible quarter section here, in section 33.

Civil War veteran Tom Stewart, the farm's first owner
COURTESY OF PAM ANDERSON, MADISON

Thomas Jefferson Stewart, the son of Solomon J. Stewart and Sally Ann Stewart, was born March 4, 1846, on a farm near Rose, New York. Tom's family had joined other New York friends in Springwater Township in Waushara County sometime between 1852 and 1860. Tom volunteered for duty in the Civil War on January 18, 1864, when he was not quite eighteen years old, and became a part of the 35th Regiment Infantry, Company F.[1]

Civil War records indicate that Tom was injured five months later. Sergeant William Striedy reported: "On the 15th of June, 1864, while in the line of duty and without fault or improper conduct on his part, at or near Port Hudson, State of Louisiana said soldier [Thomas Stewart] incurred an injury or strain while he was assisting in loading the wagons containing the Regimental equipment on to a boat to go to Morgan Bend, Louisiana. He was working with a detail of men under my charge when the wheels of one of the wagons dropped off the gang plank and he was lifting to help get it back on again. Then all at once, I saw he was hurt in some way by his looks and he said, 'Sir, I am hurt; it makes me sick.' I told him he had better go on the boat and lie down, which he did. When we got to Morganzia, I took him to the regimental hospital and [he] was afterward sent to hospital at New Orleans."[2]

Tom Stewart was in a New Orleans hospital again from August 10 through 15, 1864, this time with diarrhea "caused by drinking Mississippi River water . . . and marsh water there being no other to have at that time."[3] Tom was sick again in September and October of 1864 and was absent from his military duties. He recovered enough to continue serving with his unit and was mustered out on March 15, 1866, at Brownsville, Texas.[4] Tom received a disability pension of four dollars per month "on account of disease of urinary organs."

Tom Stewart turned twenty-one in March 1867 and staked his claim on April 30. The Homestead Act required that Tom move onto his property within six months of filing his claim. He had to build a house—a log cabin would suffice—and he had to actively farm the property, which meant growing crops. Thanks to his two years of military duty, he would own his land in only three years if he met these requirements.[5]

Tom built a cabin and other buildings on the south side of the wagon trail that split the quarter section in half. He started clearing land that first spring. Much of the sandy acres were covered with black oak, hazel brush, and stunted oak. Big bluestem grass grew in the open areas, as tall as a man in many places. Big bluestem sends its roots deep into the sandy soil, allowing it to reach moisture and withstand the dry, hot summers common in this part of Wisconsin. With his team of oxen, Tom pulled out the smaller oak trees, first shoveling soil away from the bottom of each tree until the tangled mass of roots was exposed and then hooking a heavy logging chain around each trunk and to the ox yoke. Slowly the chain tightened as the oxen pushed into their yokes. The oak roots cracked as the animals strained, and the stunted oak slowly tipped over and emerged from the sandy soil.

When he had several trees dug out, Tom dragged them into huge piles and set them ablaze. The smoke from Tom Stewart's fires could be seen for miles around, but no one was concerned. Many other farmers were clearing land they had purchased from the government. Everyone was burning brush and trees.

When he had a patch of ground cleared, Tom hired the team of Ike Woodward and William Henry Jenks, who went from farm to farm with their breaking plow and oxen to open new land. The two partners each owned two yoke of oxen (eight animals total), and together they owned the massive breaking plow, which had a white oak beam two feet thick and eighteen feet long, strong enough to absorb the shock of the plow hitting stones and tree roots. The plow's moldboard was five feet long and cut a furrow

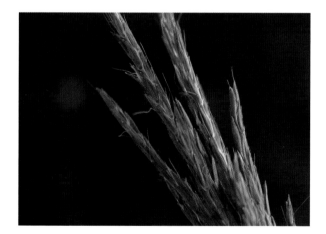

Big bluestem grass covered much of the farm before the land was first plowed.

twenty inches wide and eight or nine inches deep through the virgin soil. This moldboard was constructed to turn over soil never before disturbed—and big bluestem sod, with its thick, tough tangle of roots, was especially difficult to plow. (Farmers used a short, less powerful moldboard plow once the land was broken.)

Settlers used this type of breaking plow to turn grassy, never-before-plowed prairies.
SEARS, ROEBUCK CATALOG, 1908, FROM THE AUTHOR'S COLLECTION

The breaking plow was sturdy—and so were the plowmen. Woodward and Jenks took turns holding the plow day after day, from early spring until freeze-up, as they broke new land on farms all over Rose Township.

It took ten oxen to pull the plow. When they came to Tom Stewart's homestead, Jenks and Woodward hooked their oxen to the plow and added Tom Stewart's pair. The plow slowly turned the heavy sod, leaving golden-brown soil ready for the harrow and drag. The fresh smell of newly broken soil hinted at the untapped productivity and crops—especially wheat and potatoes—that would grow where once there was prairie and scrub oak.

Tom Stewart cleared enough land that first year to make a living from his crops. His main crop was likely wheat. Wheat was the premier crop throughout central and southern Wisconsin back as far as the 1840s, when large numbers of New Englanders and northern European immigrants began pouring into the state. The rich, never-before-plowed land yielded as much as twenty to twenty-five bushels per acre. Wisconsin rose from being the nation's ninth wheat producer in 1850 to second in 1860.[6]

But by the late 1860s Wisconsin's wheat production had begun an irrevocable decline. Many of the pioneers from New England and upper New York State had come to Wisconsin because of depleted agricultural lands back east; now these pioneer farmers were doing the same

Wisconsin farmers harvesting wheat with an early reaper, photographed in the 1870s by Andreas Larsen Dahl

Woven wire fence once formed a lane for livestock to travel from the Coombeses' barnyard to the pond.

Chapter 7

John, Ina, and Weston Coombes

"Another night like the last one and we'll be buyin' new thermometers."

INA COOMBES

After Tom Stewart sold out and moved away, a long succession of owners worked our farm for a few years and moved on. Joseph and Laura Hursh, who bought one hundred acres in 1877, sold to William Hursh in 1886, who sold to George P. Walker in 1900.[1] By that year, sixteen years after its founding, Wild Rose had eighty residents and boasted a water-powered gristmill and a school. One writer noted, "Charles A. Smart is postmaster and proprietor of the only general store. The mill is owned by James Larson. Mrs. Mary Gordon keeps a hotel. George A. Sage has a blacksmith and wagon shop, S. G. Abbott is resident physician and dentist." [2]

George P. Walker sold the farm to T. H. Patterson in 1904. Patterson, a land investor and Civil War veteran, had built a new fifty-by-one-hundred-foot, two-story brick store in Wild Rose in 1900. It was the largest building in the village.

There is no evidence that Patterson ever lived on the property he bought from Walker. Philo Darling, under a land contract (a lease arrangement) to Patterson, moved onto the place in the spring of 1904. That April, Wild Rose was incorporated as a village.[3] By the following year, eight Chicago and Northwestern passenger and freight trains would stop each day in Wild Rose, four heading north and four south.[4]

On January 17, 1904, T. H. Patterson sold the farm to D. R. Bowen for one thousand dollars. Bowen in turn entered into a land contract with Gordon Darling, who moved onto the

PART II

Roshara

An abandoned town road cuts through the farm from east to west.

Chapter 8

◇◇◇◇◇◇◇◇◇◇◇◇◇◇◇◇◇◇◇◇◇◇◇

Lay of the Land

"The woods are lovely, dark and deep,
But I have promises to keep,
and miles to go before I sleep."

Robert Frost

When facing something new, Dad always said, check the lay of the land. In other words, find out as much as you can about what you are considering. After my brothers' and my purchase of the old Coombes place from my dad, I set out to literally check the lay of the land, to walk its acres, climb its hills, and check its boundaries—to look at the trees, grasses, and wildflowers, and the remnants of its history.

In the two years that my dad owned the land, the family had done little with it. We hunted there, and hiked to the pond on occasion, but little else. When my brothers, Donald and Darrel, and I bought the land from our father for one dollar in 1966, the three of us owned it together, with no legal division of the property. My brothers agreed I could have the buildings— at that time the barn, granary, and pump house had been taken off the tax rolls as worthless.

On a sunny October day in 1966, I set out on a hike to the west of the old buildings, past the massive black willow trees that form a windbreak for the farmstead. Branches thrust this way and that, as willow trees will do. The shaggy limbs had not yet dropped their leaves. The Coombes family had planted these trees as saplings. Now some of the grayish, deeply furrowed trunks were three or more feet across.

I walked across a two-acre field to a rather steep hill that dipped down to the pond. The oaks in the woods to the north were in full fall splendor, their leaves a riot of browns, reds,

Fall brings a collage of color to Roshara.

and tans shouting for attention. The rich smell of autumn, of dead grass and fallen oak leaves, hung in the air.

The hill was deeply cut with gullies caused by heavy rains. (The Coombes family had put a stop to the washing when they planted black willow trees on the hill in 1911, at the same time they planted the willow windbreak west of the buildings.) Sandy soil, as all the farmers who've owned this land know, is extremely fragile. Wind picks it up and moves it, and heavy rains rip gullies in its surface when the grade is steep.

I followed the remnants of a woven wire fence along the farm's northern boundary to the pond in the valley. The bright yellow of maples and aspen trees that ring the valley provided a stark contrast to the clear blue sky. Giant cottonwoods, three feet in diameter and more than sixty feet tall, grew on the edge of the pond. Their yellow leaves shook nervously as a slight breeze from the west washed across the pond's surface. It was easy to see that this unnamed pond was much larger at one time, as no trees grew where the water level had once been. More than a hundred feet of dry land stretched from the present water line to the level the pond had once reached. Gazing into the water, I saw minnows swimming and noticed where muskrats had burrowed into the pond's bank. I scared a green frog from its perch on a lily pad. Deer tracks had punched into the mud near the water; a deer had come for a drink earlier this day. And the handlike paw print of a raccoon showed it had been at the pond in search of breakfast. The smells of fall near water are pungent with dead and dying vegetation preparing for the long rest of winter.

Walking around the pond to the south, I saw more huge gullies cut in a steep side hill. Oak, aspen, and birch trees grew in the gullies, some of which were so deep you could hide a small building in them.

I climbed the hill west of the pond, still following the farm's north boundary. I walked among gigantic oak trees; their growth testified to the extra moisture and richer soil near the pond. Their leaves, some past full color, were just beginning to fall. I found John Coombes's wire fence nailed to trees here and there in the woods, some of the rusty wire torn loose by falling branches and heavy snows. The fence defined the farm's boundary and kept the Coombes cattle from roaming into the big woods to the north. In several places a tree had grown around the wires, which stuck out on either side of the trunk like thin, rusty handles. According to Dad, this grove of oak and aspen trees had once been a potato patch; he remembered helping John Coombes with the harvest some twenty or more years ago.

Oak leaves add to the panorama.

As I continued my journey west, the elevation continued to increase. At the northwest corner of the property, I could see the top of Mt. Morris, one of the tallest hills in Waushara County, about eight miles to the east.

Now I turned south, picking my way along the western boundary of the farm, along another fencerow with rusty wire and broken fence posts. A few hundred yards beyond the boundary line I spotted the foundation of what had been the Stickles farm (circa 1905). Stickles had owned the 160-acre quarter section north of my place. I did not know the present owners. I could make out the fieldstone walls of the barn—all that remained—and the foundation where the house once stood. The walking trail that begins at my farmstead and goes straight west had once been a town road that connected the Stickles farm with the rest of the world.

The remnants of a barbwire fence mark the northern boundary of the farm.
Oak trees have grown around the wire that was nailed to them.

I hiked along the western boundary, across a field of maybe five acres, once farmed but now abandoned. Here and there grew jack pine trees, which are native to the area, and Scotch pine, which are not. Christmas tree growers introduced Scotch pine to the area several years ago, and the pine seeds had spread widely.

I found hazelnut bushes, some hanging with ripe hazelnuts in their chocolate brown covers, and evergreen juniper bushes. Both hazelnut and juniper are natives.

At the southern boundary I turned east and walked first through a small grove of black and bur oak trees and then through a scattering of black cherry trees, jack pine, more Scotch pine, and another row of black willow planted as a windbreak. I emerged on a large, open field, twenty acres or more, that had once been a cornfield. It hadn't been plowed for several years, and I saw a scattering of Scotch and jack pine and even a few box elder trees that had self-seeded. The field was a garden of wildflowers. I found blue spiderwort and the small red flowers of sheep sorrel. Both grow well on acid, sandy soils. Some alternative medicine advocates claim that a tea made from sheep sorrel is antidiarrheal, anti-inflammatory, and antioxidant. Native people often referred to sheep sorrel as sour week or sour grass.

Patches of hawkweed were everywhere, some yellow, some orange. Black-eyed Susan grew here and there, now a couple months past its peak flowering time. Some botanists consider this beautiful and tough little flower, which will grow in the most difficult of situations, the most common of all wildflowers.

I spotted several stalks of common mullein growing in the field. Mullein is an impressive wildflower; some stalks will grow as high as five or six feet, even on sandy soil. Mullein is biennial, which means it lives two years. The first year it produces a rosette of yellow flowers; the second it sends up its tall stalk, which produces seeds. It's known as a pioneer plant, as it is one of the first to grow after soil has been disturbed. Generally classified as

Black-eyed Susans

an herb, mullein is not native to the United States; early European settlers brought the plant with them because of its medicinal qualities. Pioneers made a tea from the leaves to treat colds and used the flowers and roots to soothe ailments from earaches to coughs. Sometimes the leaves were applied to skin to sooth sunburn. Dad always called it Indian tobacco; the big, velvety leaves resemble tobacco leaves, and some claim that when smoked they provide a respiratory stimulant.

Goldenrods grew everywhere in my wildflower field, many in their full fall yellow finery. They grow in patches, mostly in hollows where the soil is a little richer and holds a bit more moisture. We had goldenrods on the home farm as well, and in the winter, before we set off for a day of ice fishing, we stuffed our pockets with goldenrod galls, little balls that grow on the goldenrod stem. Slicing open the gall with a jackknife, we'd find a little grub nestled there, insulated from the cold of winter. Bluegills, perch, and other panfish savored this tasty bait.

At one end of the field I found a patch of common milkweeds, their big, brown pods about to burst and release hundreds of seeds to fly away on the little gossamer parachutes attached to each. Without milkweeds we'd have few Monarch butterflies, as this plant is one of their primary food sources. The milky sap inside the milkweed's leaves and stem contains toxic cardiac glycosides. When the Monarch caterpillar eats the milkweed leaves, the glycosides

Ripe milkweed pods await a strong wind to distribute their seeds.

remain in its body, making the caterpillar poisonous to predators. (The adult butterfly continues to have glycosides in its body, making it poisonous to predators as well.) As I walked among the milkweeds, I remembered that during World War II my fellow country school students and I collected milkweed pods by the sackful and sent them away to become stuffing for life jackets worn by sailors and airmen.

I ambled across the big open field, thinking about Weston Coombes with his team of horses plowing, discing, and planting these acres, hoping for a good harvest but taking what he would get from this sandy soil.

The eastern edge of this field drops off quickly in a long, steep hill covered with Scotch and jack pine and a large patch of big bluestem grass. At the bottom of this hill, I pictured how these long valleys became the glacial streams that carried excess meltwater to the south and east, draining the area and forming the hills and valleys. I pondered the huge boulders scattered on our hilltops, wondered about their sources and how many thousands of miles they traveled embedded in a wall of ice before being left behind as the glacier receded.

At the top of another long, sandy hill, so barren that no grass grew there, I found only mosses and lichens. Along the top edge of the hill grew a north-south row of white pines forming another windbreak. The gentle breeze rustled the soft needles of these native trees, which grow in much of central and northern Wisconsin. Later I learned from Dad that John Coombes planted these pines during the 1930s, when drought plagued much of the country, including central Wisconsin. White pines grow quickly on sandy soil, and the trees blocked the dry winds that incessantly tore at the land, lifting the soil in huge dusty clouds and taking the fertility with it. As I walked along the rows of pines I saw huge mounds of soil piled against their trunks, evidence that the trees had served well in stopping the erosion.

On the other side of the windbreak was another field of seven or eight acres where corn had once been planted. I found remnants of decaying cornstalks and saw where the plowman had left his mark with dead furrows and back furrows, the depressions and humps formed when the plow piles two furrows on top of each other. These furrows cut across the length of the field, according to how the plowman made them with his one-bottom walking plow pulled by a team of draft horses. I thought again of Weston Coombes, walking behind his plow, one foot in the furrow, the horses' reins draped across his shoulders, his hands gripping the handles of the plow. The sandy soil must have turned readily with no stones in the path of the plow, making the work relatively easy—if plowing with a one-bottom plow can ever be called easy.

The circa 1914 Rose Township plat map shows the locations of the original farm buildings.

ATLAS AND FARMERS' DIRECTORY OF WAUSHARA COUNTY, WISCONSIN, CIRCA 1914

Soon I was on 15th Road, still a gravel road in 1966 just as it had been in 1852 or 1853, when the first trail plunged through this area along the section lines made by land surveyors. In a little field immediately south of the driveway into our farm, I looked for remnants of where Tom Stewart built the first farmstead in 1867. The buildings still appear on a map in the township's circa 1914 plat book. Now all I could see was a flat area on top of a little rise, likely the place where the first cabin and barn had stood.

Hills and valleys, gullies and rusty wire fence, wildflowers and grasses, white pines and black oaks, remnants of cornfields, memories of cow pastures, high ground and pond—all are a part of the lay of the land at this old farm. All speak of its history.

Pump house boards scorched in the 1959 fire remain charred to this day.

Chapter 9

◇◇◇◇◇◇◇◇◇◇◇◇◇◇◇◇◇◇◇◇◇◇

Gray Buildings

"The cabin had not been built for summer comfort or view. It had no real-estate value."
Sigurd Olson

Having completed my survey of my new land that October day in 1966, I turned my attention to the old, gray buildings. What stories would the remnants of the house and these decrepit old farm buildings reveal?

To the south of the barn, granary, and pump house, I saw the remnants of a barbwire fence with crooked posts, rusting wire, and a corner post braced with diagonal wooden poles. The fence surrounded a small field that Weston Coombes had used to pasture his small herd of Guernsey cows and the team of skinny horses that powered his rusty farm equipment.

The pump house overlooked another fenced field, once the Coombes barnyard. A few box elder trees lined the barnyard fence, volunteers that sprouted and grew rapidly after the Coombes family moved away. The pump house sheltered the pump and well that provided water for the farm. The south side of the pump house's pine siding was scorched and burned, a reminder of the fire that destroyed the farmhouse a few years earlier. A windmill once straddled the pump house. Perched at the top of the windmill tower, twenty or more feet up, had been a big metal wheel with fans designed to catch the slightest breeze. The wind would spin the wheel, which moved a pump rod up and down. The pump rod moved within a two-inch pipe that was pounded into the ground sixty-plus feet down to water. As the rod went up and down, a valve at the end opened and closed, moving water up the pipe and then

Artifacts left in the pump house from an earlier day, when farmers saved everything, including old nails

Chapter 10

⬦⬦⬦⬦⬦⬦⬦⬦⬦⬦⬦⬦⬦⬦⬦⬦⬦

Pump House

"John Coombes, Wild Rose, Wis. N.W. Bag.
In case of loss notify Blue Valley Creamery Company."
BRASS PLATE ON FIVE-GALLON CREAM CAN

Every building has a story. The old pump house on my farm is no exception. John Coombes made the building twelve feet wide, sixteen feet long, and twelve feet tall at the peak of its gable roof. The side walls are eight feet high. Whether he was aware of it or not, Coombes was building for the future when he constructed the building on a poured concrete wall. Many farmers, especially in the poorer sections of the Upper Midwest, found some big fieldstones and piled them under the corners of a building for support. That had to be good enough.

It is not difficult to picture John and his son, Weston, mixing mud (as preparing concrete was called in those days). So many shovels full of Portland cement, so many shovels full of screened sand—the wood-frame screen was tucked up under the roof, where it remains today. Pour in some water from the newly dug well and mix it with a hoe until it turns a dark gray and pours—but just barely.

Before they mixed the concrete, they made forms from two-inch planks that they braced with two-by-four lumber. The forms would hold the wet concrete in place until it dried and became hard. All this took some thinking and planning, for the pump house is not on level ground. On the west side of the building the concrete foundation is only six inches or so high; on the east side it is three feet high. Perhaps John Coombes had the savvy to plan all of this so the building would be straight with the world—a phrase country people used when describing

Thunderstorms added a challenge to camping at the farm.

Chapter 13

Cleanup

"I will not sleep in the same room with a mouse."
RUTH APPS

The first few summer vacations after we bought the farm we pitched an old umbrella tent under the shade of the big black willow trees that had served as a windbreak for the farmstead. The kids were little tykes at the time, enjoying every minute of their new camping experience.

We had added a new building to the farmstead that made camping possible, the first new building on the site since 1912. No matter that it was a two-holer outhouse, it was new, and it smelled new. An employee of the Wild Rose Lumberyard built it for us and hauled it out to the farm. The kids and I spent an afternoon painting it. By late afternoon, everything was brown— the outhouse, the grass around it, and of course the kids. All brown. Ruth was not especially happy and wondered how I had let the painting get so out of hand that even the faces of the kids were brown. I just smiled and reminded her that the outhouse was painted. She dropped the topic.

We lit our campsite with a Coleman gasoline lantern and cooked our meals on a Coleman gas stove. Mosquitoes menaced us some evenings, but camping was mostly a pleasant experience, with a few exceptions.

Our nearly daily afternoon treat after working to clean up the years of clutter accumulated in the Coombes yard was to go swimming. One sultry day in August 1968 I noticed a solid line of thunderstorms building in the western sky as we drove home from the Kusel Lake beach, a few miles east of Wild Rose.

A hand saw of the type Ole Knutson used to help transform the granary into a cabin

Chapter 14

~~~~~~~~~~~~~~~~~~~~~

Cabin Building

"Dad, is this worth a whole-pail shower?"

THE APPS CHILDREN

"First thing to do is fix the roof," Ole Knutson had said when he inspected the granary. "No sense doing anything else when the roof leaks."

During my summer vacation in 1968, I pounded a new roof on the old granary. It was blistering hot, and even hotter on the granary roof. Each day I started roofing early in the morning and had to stop by noon when the temperature shot into the nineties. Total cost for the shingles: seventy-six dollars. I put them over wood shingles that were as old as the granary itself.

As I worked on the roof that summer, where it was hot but quiet, I couldn't stop thinking about the turmoil that was going on in Madison at the University of Wisconsin campus and around the country.

On April 4 Dr. Martin Luther King Jr. was murdered in Memphis. He was just thirty-nine years old. On April 5 rioting erupted in Chicago, Washington, D.C., Detroit—in nearly every major U.S. city. Yellow flames lit the city skies, and dark smoke billowed upward. Many states called out National Guard units to attempt to restore order. Federal troops ringed the White House; a machine gun was positioned on the White House lawn.

Ten thousand University of Wisconsin–Madison students assembled for memorial services on Bascom Hill, and fifteen thousand marched down State Street and around the Capitol Square. President Lyndon Johnson announced he would not run for a second term

Stiff aster, a common prairie flower

Chapter 15

✧✧✧✧✧✧✧✧✧✧✧✧✧✧✧✧✧

Roshara

"You've got to give the place a name."
Isabelle Downie, *Waushara Argus* reader

In the spring of 1967 I began writing a freelance column for the *Waushara Argus*, a weekly newspaper for Waushara County and adjoining counties. In "Outdoor Notebook" I wrote about the environment and nature, country living, and rural history.

Our family's adventures at the farm became regular topics. I wrote about tree planting and brush clearing. I described the pond in summer and in winter. I wrote about skiing and sledding on our hilly acres, and about butterflies and squirrels and rabbits and wildflowers of many descriptions. I chronicled the children's encounters with bumblebees, garter snakes, and field mice. As readers became familiar with our farm and what we were doing here, they began asking for the name of the place. We variously referred to it as "the farm" or our "country place."

"You've got to give the place a name," Mrs. Isabelle Downie of Wautoma, who owned a small resort on Silver Lake, told me one day. "Town of Rose Farm is no name."

I tossed the idea back to the column readers. In an early October column I wrote, "I've got a problem and I think you can help. I need a name for our Town of Rose farm. And I will give a new bird guidebook to the person who suggests a name we like." I told readers we had thought of several names already; Ruth had suggested that we call the place Aching Acres in honor of our many days of hard work here. But we hadn't thought of the perfect name.

PART III

Living on the Farm

Old road in fall

Chapter 16

Old Road

"Two roads diverged in a wood, and I—
I took the one less traveled by,
and that has made all the difference."

ROBERT FROST

I've always been drawn to country roads—the kind that twist and turn and go up hills and down as they follow the lay of the land rather than plow straight ahead as modern-day roads are prone to do. Just such a country road trails by our farm. It is a mostly north-and-south road that follows survey lines, cutting section 33 in half until it drops down and makes a wide sweep around the east end of Chain O' Lake before climbing and heading north once more. It intersects with another country road, now County Highway A, that for years was known as the "old Indian Road" and was so noted by a government land surveyor in 1851.

Country roads were and are maintained according to their designation—town roads, county roads, state roads, and federal roads, each maintained by their respective governmental stewards. The higher the governmental designation, the greater the traffic, the straighter and wider the road, and the more boring the ride. On these more "modern" roads you can travel from here to there more quickly, which seems to be the goal of most people these days.

I learned by studying old plat maps that a town road once ran right through our farm, east to west. It intersected with the north-and-south road that runs by our farm. This abandoned town road once connected with another, now long-abandoned road to the west of our farm, providing easy access to the Ed Stickles farm. This mysterious road, no longer mapped, no longer maintained, and no longer traveled except by my family and me, follows the quarter-

Walking west on
the old road

It has never been given a name but always referred to as "the pond." On some maps it appears, just barely; on others it is missing entirely. Yet it is a central feature of our farm, where something new is happening nearly every day of the year.

This small body of water, about five acres when the water table is high, is a mysterious, mythical part of our place. It is ever changing and always the same. It provides sanctuary for hundreds of birds—shelter in a storm for migrating ducks, geese, and even a pair of swans on one occasion. This is where all the wildlife in the area comes for water when rain is short and the land is parched.

For me it is also a spiritual place, especially on quiet mornings when wisps of fog lift from the still water and gather in little tongues that float on the surface. And in the evening, too, when the last robin sings and the water turns from blue to black as the sun slips behind the western hills. The stillness provides a time for uninterrupted reflection on my assorted problems and challenges and happy things as well. This is often the first place I go in the morning and the last place in the evening.

This dead tree is evidence of much higher pond levels.

As I stand by the pond on a rainy afternoon, each drop of rain creates a tiny whirlpool on the pond's surface and makes a tinkling sound like someone gently touching the upper-octave keys on a piano. By contrast, rain drips with a brusque thwack-thwack-thwack from the oaks and poplars and birches that line the shore.

Sitting quietly near the pond on a warm spring evening, I sometimes see deer coming down from the hills and woods for water, perhaps a doe with a pair of fawns still in their spotted coats but playful and unmindful of mama doe's direction. Or a mother raccoon and her brood, the little masked rascals carefully dipping their paws into the water, learning the ways of their parents.

If I am fortunate, and I often am, a mallard hen moves out of the rushes followed by a line of baby ducks, paddling furiously to keep up with mama but staying in a straight line behind her. All but one. There is always one that has another idea, another direction in mind. Mother duck turns around and swims back and chastises the naughty youngster, or so it appears.

The pond is a mysterious place all seasons of the year.

The pond's water level fluctuates with the years. In 2007 the pond was at the lowest level we've seen since 1967.

The pond is roughly ten thousand years old, just a youngster in geologic time, formed when a huge chunk of ice was buried by the last glacier to visit the area and then melted, leaving a depression that filled with water. It has neither an inlet nor an outlet but is fed by several springs on its south and west sides that bubble up year-round. Ours is a water table pond, which means its level goes up and down based on natural cycles of the water table—a great underground river of water known as an aquifer.

When we first acquired the farm, the pond was but a marshy area with little open water. Dad said, "I think we can improve this little lake." Although I was skeptical, I didn't say anything. My skepticism about improving on nature goes deep. Most of the time "improvement" results in further degradation.

What Dad had in mind was bringing in a dredge and deepening one end of the pond. With permission and some cost sharing from the government for wetland improvement, Dad hired a man with a dredge to dig out the mucky bottom of one end of the pond to a depth of eight or ten feet—and in so doing uncovered springs buried for years by several feet of soil that had washed into the pond from the nearby fields. The springs were an unintended bonus, and within a few years the pond was three times its previous size.

Over the forty years that we have owned the place, the pond level has gone up and down significantly at least three times. At its highest point, as recently as ten years ago, the pond had created an island with water flowing around the west side of a little knob of ground on which grew several oak and poplar trees. The high water killed birch and poplars all around the shore as each year the pond grew larger and larger. The little pond formed when Dad had the original dredged became a part of the larger pond. A survey post that had been on high ground was now several feet below the surface.

The pond is now at one of its low points in this mysterious water table cycle. The little pond to the southwest is nearly dry. The north end of the main pond has become marshlike again; new seedling trees once more grow where there had been water. The island is an island no more, merely a high point along the shore.

The pond is not only filled with bullheads, turtles, frogs, and assorted other water creatures, it is teeming with memories. Our three children spent many weekends and vacations swimming in its sometimes-murky waters, looking for creatures along its shores, canoeing every nook and cranny, fishing for bluegills, waiting quietly for deer to come for a drink on a warm summer evening, listening to the bullfrog chorus of loud "harrumphs" on an August night as darkness engulfed the valley that surrounds this little body of water.

The pond is also a place for surprises. One early spring morning, grandson Josh and I walked quietly to the east side, to the shore just down the hill from the cabin. I told Josh to walk as quietly as possible and not to talk, for the sounds of our approaching would spook any wildlife in the area. He nodded his understanding, and we shuffled quietly along the path, through the dewy grass of morning. The pond was as smooth and shiny as a tabletop. I caught a movement in the rushes on the far side, and I motioned for Josh to stop. A sandhill crane, a long-legged, four-foot-tall gray bird with a red cap, emerged from the tall grass and stood on the shore. We watched in awe. Josh had never seen a sandhill crane, probably had never seen any bird this large, especially this close.

Without warning, the crane began its mating dance. The huge bird flapped its wings and lifted its long legs high, trying to impress a mate we did not see. Watching this extraordinary event with my grandson was a highlight of the year for me. I couldn't wait to hear Josh exclaim to his mother, "Guess what we saw, Mom?"

Sandhill cranes hold a conversation at the pond.

Months later, on a cold, dark night in December, Josh, his brother Ben, their mother, and I walked through the dark to the pond, along the trail that threaded past naked oaks and poplars that were near invisible in the black night. I carried a flashlight but didn't turn it on, telling my grandsons that their eyes would adjust to the dark and they would be able to see their way in a few minutes. They did not believe me until minutes later they discovered that what had been black and invisible now had shape and form.

At the pond we walked on the smooth ice, the kids running, sliding, falling down, laughing, giggling, getting up, and falling down again. I shined the flashlight down through the ice and watched the beam filter to the bottom of the pond, where pond plants grew green and alive. Josh and Ben were amazed that light could penetrate ice.

We walked closer to shore, and I pointed out a muskrat run, where cunning muskrats had burrowed into the bank and formed an entryway into the pond. I saw the excitement on the boys' faces as I described how muskrats live in the pond year-round and what these little rodents eat and how well they can swim.

I was in the middle of my discussion of muskrats—interest was clearly waning on the part of my young audience—when it happened. A muskrat appeared under the ice and entered its tunnel. I turned the flashlight beam on this underwater swimmer. The reality of seeing overpowered my efforts at explanation. "Wow!" I heard. "Cool." Not often are my stories punctuated at just the right moment with the main actor coming on stage for an appearance!

We walked back to the middle of the pond, where the water was deepest. The boys' mother asked if the ice was safe out there, and I said that it was, for it was several inches thick. More sliding and falling down and giggling. The cold north wind was still that night, and a thin thread of a moon was visible in the black sky. Our sounds of merriment echoed in the valley as the pond waited for spring and young boys did what young boys have done for years—having fun without the need for equipment.

Without warning there was a loud noise, a sound like a rifle shot that pierced the quiet and echoed across the valley. At almost the same moment a crack formed in the ice, rushing past where the boys were playing. They heard the sound and saw the crack and knew for sure the ice was breaking. The boys yelled and ran for shore, their mother hurrying behind them. On shore I tried to explain that it was no more than a pressure crack, an expansion crack in the ice. "Think of the ice as talking to you," I said. My words meant little to boys now afraid of returning to their play. Soon, though, the boys had forgotten the loud cracking and were reluctant to return to the cabin—until they remembered that there waited hot chocolate and a grandmother eager to listen to their stories.

For me, sitting alone by the pond on a quiet evening or walking on the ice in winter, when the northwest wind sends slivers of snow hurrying across in ever-changing patterns, has meaning that transcends the words I use to describe the experience. The pond is one of the places on my farm where nature reaches into the depths of who I am, what I believe, and what I value. It is a quiet teacher, a patient listener, and a steady force.

This old apple tree is the sole survivor of an orchard likely planted by Tom Stewart in 1867 or 1868.

Chapter 18

◇◇◇◇◇◇◇◇◇◇◇◇◇◇◇◇◇◇

Apple Trees, Lilacs, and Daylilies

"In the dooryard fronting an old farm-house near the white-washed palings,
Stands the lilac-bush tall-growing with heart-shaped leaves of rich green,
With many a pointed blossom rising delicate, with the perfume strong I love,
With every leaf a miracle. . . ."
Walt Whitman

The tree looks like an old man, bald on top and with tufts of white on each side of his head. The analogy is about more than mere appearance, for this tree is extremely old as apple trees go, especially fruit-bearing trees. It grows alongside a little field to the south of the cabin, not far from where Tom Stewart built his original log house and barn and perhaps other log buildings I can only guess about. I want to estimate the age of the apple tree. I know Tom Stewart acquired this land in 1867; I know that he originally came from Wayne County, New York; I know it was common for New Yorkers and others who settled in what was known as Western country to bring apple trees and other plants with them. Apple growing was common in the East from colonial days, and like New York and New England, Wisconsin provided hospitable growing conditions for fruit trees, especially apples. Settlers like Tom Stewart commonly planted small orchards near their buildings. Thus, my guess is that this apple tree was planted in 1867 or thereabouts, making it more than 135 years old. The tree is likely the oldest living connection we have to our land's original homesteader.

When my family bought this land in 1966, four or five apple trees bordered this acre-sized field that at one time included barnyard, clothesline, vegetable garden, and perhaps some flower beds besides the log buildings—but I'm guessing again. What I know for sure is that this apple tree is so old that its main trunk is dead and broken off. Four or five years ago I found the top of the tree in a field, cracked off in a windstorm. It's the end of the tree, I thought. But it lived on, the remaining center trunk now mostly dead and scraggly where the broken trunk thrusts upward. There was enough life left in the old original trunk to send out side branches, and those branches continue to bloom and bear fruit.

Early settlers to Rose Township, many of them from upstate New York, brought with them daylilies, lilacs, and apple trees.

Tom Stewart may have also brought daylilies, orange and yellow ones, from New York, as daylilies grow in profusion around our old pump house and in another patch a few yards farther south. Tom's daughter, Ina, probably moved the daylilies when the family abandoned the log buildings and the old farmstead and constructed new buildings a few hundred yards to the north. But even as the old buildings fell into disrepair, the daylilies continued on undaunted.

Native to China, Japan, Korea, and eastern Siberia, daylilies were cultivated long before the birth of Christ. Some early Chinese records claim that daylilies were used to relieve physical as well as mental pain. The juice extracted from daylily roots supposedly quieted the heart, lungs, liver, kidneys, and stomach; benefited the mind; strengthened willpower; reduced worry and body weight; and brightened the eyes—all in addition to providing a splash of color to Chinese gardens. What more could one ask of this lowly plant?

The daylily's botanical name is *Hemerocallis*, from the Greek *hemera* (day) and *kallos* (beauty). Daylilies made their way to Europe along with spices imported from the Orient. By the 1500s daylilies were popular in Europe, and they crossed the Atlantic with the Pilgrims. The tawny orange daylily moved west with the settlers and became known to some as the homestead lily.[1]

Lilacs grow in front of the black willow windbreak, no doubt planted by the Coombes family after they constructed their new buildings. In late May they flower, deep purple, lighter purple, and white. The scent of lilac on a warm spring evening is one of the treats we look forward to each year, unless a late frost has killed the flowering buds, which happens one year in five. But even with a frost some of the lilacs will manage to bloom and let us know they are

Apple blossoms appear each spring on the old apple tree that once stood behind Tom Stewart's farm buildings.

there with their sweet aroma. We always have a big bouquet of lilacs on the cabin table when they are in season, their subtle spring smell mixing with aromas of wood smoke from our wood-burning kitchen range.

Lilacs originated in Turkey; their name comes from the Arabic *laylak* or the Persian *nylac*, meaning blue. The botanical name *Syringa* is from the Greek *syrinx*, a pipe. The shrub can grow to twenty feet and has pithy stems that can be hollowed out. The Turks apparently used the stems as pipes.

Lilacs are long-lived and require little or no care. Like apple trees and daylilies, lilac roots made their way west with settlers. "American settlers planted lilacs in front of farmhouse doors, not for usefulness but for beauty, while they struggled to make a new life in the wilderness. Sometimes the slowly cleared fields, the houses, and the walls were no more permanent than those who made them, but the lilacs remained by the ghost porches, leading nowhere."[2] Today it is easy to spot a former farmstead, even if all the buildings are gone. Look for a clump of lilacs. They are tough and persistent.

Our apple tree, daylilies, and lilacs are living connections to the history of our land, reminding us year after year of earlier days and the people who farmed these sandy acres before us—people who enjoyed the smell of lilacs on a warm spring evening, the splash of daylily orange in early summer, and the sweet taste of fresh apples in fall.

Chapter 19

Wildlife

"Who cooks for you? Who cooks for you-allllll?"

BARRED OWL

A wild turkey will lay ten to twelve eggs, but because the nest is on the ground,
predators will take many of them.

She flicked her ears back and forth, her head high as she tried to catch my scent. Now she turned away and walked back into the tall prairie grass, still keeping an eye on me. She circled, coming closer and closer. Now she was only thirty-five or so yards away, the prairie grass nearly to the top of her back. We both stared.

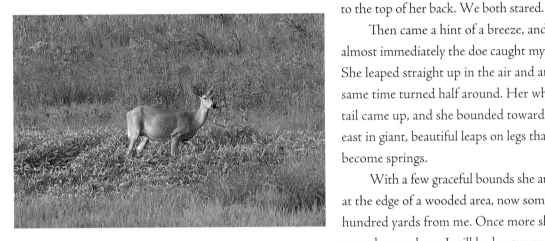

A whitetail deer feeds in the field next to the pond.

Then came a hint of a breeze, and almost immediately the doe caught my scent. She leaped straight up in the air and at the same time turned half around. Her white tail came up, and she bounded toward the east in giant, beautiful leaps on legs that had become springs.

With a few graceful bounds she arrived at the edge of a wooded area, now some two hundred yards from me. Once more she turned toward me; I still had not moved. She lowered her tail and snorted loudly, the sound echoing through the steamy valley. She snorted once, twice more. And then she looked for a reaction from me.

In a minute or two she slipped into the woods and disappeared. I remained motionless, and in a scant few minutes she emerged from the woods and went back to eating prairie grass. She had either forgotten I was there or decided to ignore this motionless guy on top of the hill who insisted on watching a lady eat her supper.

Over the years I've seen many deer at Roshara, but seldom this close to me. I learned long ago that early evening is a good time for deer watching.

~~~~~~

Neither Ruth nor I are serious bird-watchers; we don't travel to exotic places with bird-watching in mind or keep lists of birds we've identified. Yet we love the birds at our farm in all seasons of the year.

Our bird season starts with March's lengthening days. The cardinals call at daybreak, their clear whistle starting my day on a high. By mid-March I hear the first ruffed grouse in the woods to the north of the farm. Its wings pound slowly at first, then more rapidly, like an old John Deere tractor. Later in the month, the first Canada geese are winging over. The "gobble, gobble" of wild turkeys—they have been quiet all winter—tells me spring is near. About the same time I hear the sandhill cranes calling, and I know they are back from their winter quarters. The sandhill crane's rattling call is one of a kind; some say the bird sounds like it has a sore throat. For me the sandhill's cry is delightful, haunting and prehistoric—a reminder of dinosaur days when giant creatures walked the earth and enormous flying creatures blotted out the sun. A pair of sandhills nests on the west side of our pond every year.

In spring we see red-winged blackbirds and killdeer at the pond, great blue herons wading along the shore looking for minnows, and the smaller green heron, with its piercing call. Mallards and wood ducks return to the pond by April. We have constructed houses for both species, on posts in the water so that predators have difficulty getting to them.

Usually on a cold, blustery day in late March we see our first robin, its feathers all fluffed up as it searches for insects on the bare, brown grass in front of the cabin. By April the migrant birds are passing through, flocks of warblers that rest in our willow trees for a few days before moving on north.

The bluebirds return in late March or early April. We put up our first bluebird houses forty years ago. Now each year we replace those that have clearly seen better times with new ones, bolted to black locust posts that we cut from the locus patch. Every year about 20 percent of our bluebird houses will have bluebirds. The rest are claimed by tree swallows.

A tree swallow pokes its head out of one of many bluebird houses at Roshara. Tree swallows often nest in unused bluebird houses.

With the arrival of May and warmer temperatures, our summer birds begin returning to the birdfeeder hanging in the white spruce just outside the cabin window. Along with the cardinals and nuthatches that overwintered, we now see rose-breasted grosbeaks, indigo buntings, mourning doves, and goldfinches.

WILDLIFE AT ROSHARA

- **badger** (*Taxidea taxus*)
- **beaver** (*Castor canadensis*)
- **black bear** (*Ursus americanus*)
- **brown bat** (*Eptesicus fuscus*)
- **coyote** (*Canis latrans*)
- **deer mouse** (*Peromyscus maniculatus*)
- **eastern chipmunk** (*Tamias striatus*)
- **eastern cottontail rabbit** (*Sylvilagus floridanus*)
- **eastern gray squirrel** (*Sciurus carolinensis*)
- **flying squirrel** (*Glaucomys sabrinus*)
- **fox squirrel** (*Sciurus niger*)
- **house mouse** (*Mus musculus*)
- **mink** (*Mustela vison*)
- **muskrat** (*Ondatra zibethica*)
- **raccoon** (*Procyon lotor*)
- **red fox** (*Vulpes vulpes*)
- **red squirrel** (*Tamiasciurus hudsonicus*)
- **river otter** (*Lutra canadensis*)
- **striped skunk** (*Mephitis mephitis*)
- **thirteen-lined ground squirrel** (striped gopher) (*Spermophilus tridecemlineatus*)
- **white-tailed deer** (*Odocoileus virginianus*)
- **woodchuck** (*Marmota monax*)

One year the Apps children found a cottontail rabbit's nest near the lilac bushes. Predators had taken all but one baby rabbit.

PHOTO FROM THE AUTHOR'S COLLECTION

Many other summer birds do not come to the feeder. Baltimore orioles build elaborate hanging nests in our willow trees, and house wrens take up residence in the little birdhouse outside the kitchen window. Their happy chatter often wakes us in the morning. Gray catbirds nest in the willows. They meow like a cat and also mimic the calls of other birds, sometimes letting loose with a delightful repertoire of mixed birdsong. Occasionally we spot a ruby-throated hummingbird flitting around the rosebush by the corner of the cabin, its filmy wings moving so rapidly we can scarcely see them.

On a hot day in summer I'll often spot a red-tailed hawk sailing over my prairie, its wings motionless as it rides the updraft thermals. I'm reminded to look for it when I hear its piercing "kee-wee" call. And on a hot, still summer night, the whip-poor-will calls its own name over and over again, sometimes ten or more times in a row. We seldom see this reclusive, ground-loving bird, but its call is unmistakable as it echoes through the valley west of the cabin and lulls us to sleep.

With the coming of fall, our summer birds begin disappearing, winging their way to warmer climes. Great skeins of Canada geese fly high overhead, their call reassuring—for some things are still right with the world as long as the geese make their seasonal migrations.

On frosty October evenings, when the sky is so clear that you could count every star, a barred owl calls from the deep woods to the north: "Who cooks for you? Who cooks for you-allllll?" Often the call is answered from a different direction. Are these love calls in the night, I wonder.

With the passing days of autumn and the first snowfall, our winter regulars begin returning to the birdfeeder, assured of something to eat when their supply of weed and wildflower seeds become buried in snowdrifts. Chickadees, friendly little birds with a black cap and a winter personality, will face whatever weather is thrown their way and joyfully sing their name over and over. They usually appear first, flying in from the protection of the lilacs near the black

willow windbreak. They sit on a lower branch of the big spruce, waiting while I fill the feeder. No matter how cold or how snowy, they always greet me with a cheery "chick-a-dee-dee-dee." Juncos, sometimes called snowbirds, appear next. With slate gray backs and whitish bellies, they gather on the ground under the feeder to eat what others have spilled. Soon we see white-breasted nuthatches, an occasional downy woodpecker, brilliant red male cardinals and the more muted females, and bluejays, often the bullies at the feeder, forcing others away while they devour what they want.

Wild turkeys have become common at the farm.

Usually at dusk, when a gray winter afternoon slowly becomes darker as the unseen sun begins to set, several wild turkeys sneak in quietly from the field to the west to feast on the feeder leavings on the ground. Later, deer will do the same thing. Turkey and deer tracks in the snow give them away when I walk by the feeder in the morning on my way to the woodshed for an armful of stove wood.

The work of a pileated woodpecker on a dead pine tree

No matter how cold or miserable a winter day, crows are always present, calling from the tops of a tall cottonwood trees near the pond, flying over the snow-covered prairie, roosting in the white pine plantation. A bird seldom praised, the crows' presence is one constant when other wild creatures are hunkered down, waiting for warmer temperatures.

Sometimes on a quiet winter morning, I hear the loud "rat-tat-tat" of a woodpecker looking for breakfast, a grub or worm in a dead tree. Several times in recent years I've watched a pileated woodpecker work. The pileated is our largest woodpecker, sixteen to nineteen inches tall with a wingspan up to thirty inches and boasting black with white neck stripes and a prominent red crest. It is a beautiful creature—and an effective wood chiseler. It not only pounds holes in dead trees (it seems to prefer pines and poplars), it chisels out rectangular holes in live trees as well, sometimes three or more inches long and an inch wide. It's easy to spot a pileated woodpecker's work; just look for a pile of wood chips gathered at the base of a tree, scattered on the white snow. But catching the bird at work is a challenge, as it is shy and prefers working out of sight. By following the sound of the pounding and creeping along quietly with binoculars in hand, I've been able to watch this woodpecker work for fifteen minutes or more before it senses me and flies off, letting go with a loud "cuk-cuk-cuk" that echoes through the woods on a cold morning.

The wild animals and birds have been our constant neighbors here. Except for a few neighborly misunderstandings, especially concerning my garden, we have gotten along well. How drab the countryside would be without them.

Chapter 20

Characters

"Glad you bought this place. Good to have a neighbor again."

FLOYD JEFFERS

Bill Boose of Wild Rose painted a picture of the farmstead in 1971.

Karner blue butterfly

Prairie and Karner Blues

"To make a prairie it takes a clover and one bee,
One clover, and a bee,
And revery. The revery alone will do,
If bees are few."
EMILY DICKINSON

We began restoring our prairie by default. When we first acquired the farm from my dad in 1966, my two brothers and I owned the one hundred acres together. We decided that the big field above the hill to the south of the pond and stretching to the farm's southern border would be an ideal location for a cornfield. The field was about fifteen acres, less hilly than much of the farm, with slightly heavier soil and rocks only here and there. No plowman wants to hear of rocks, no matter whether he farms with horses or the fanciest new mechanized equipment. Rocks break plows, bend tillage equipment, and fray the nerves of farmers.

My brothers and I asked David Kolka, a farmer neighbor and former schoolmate, if he'd be interested in planting the field with corn. We struck a deal in which he would give us a portion of the crop as rent; we hoped to take in enough money from the corn sold to pay our land taxes. The first couple years the rains came regularly, and our corn crop was average.

We planted corn for several years in the late 1960s. But then in 1970 or 1971 a low-rainfall year came along—they seem to come regularly to sandy farms—and David's corn crop was a near failure. We knew he would not get back from the corn sale what he had put into the project—time, machine, seed, and fertilizer costs. Our return on the project was near nonexistent. We amicably agreed to grow no more corn at Roshara, except for a few rows of sweet corn in the garden.

When David quit growing corn in the big field, the next season the land became a mass of weeds—ragweed, lambs quarter, foxtail, quack grass, even some thistles in the hollows. As we looked across an expanse of corn stubble and thriving weeds, we wondered if we'd made

True to its name, butterfly weed attracts many species of butterflies.

the right decision to quit working this field. Ironically, that season ample rain fell and the weeds grew abundantly, some waist high. My brothers and I were busy with our young families and our careers and paid little attention to this weed field. As farmers we had grown up fighting weeds on the home farm. We cultivated to eliminate them; we hoed them, chopped them, cut them with a scythe. Whenever there was a slack time in other farmwork, we worked at controlling weeds. Now we had allowed acres of weeds to grow undisturbed, to thrive without threat of hoe or sickle. In this field at least, the weeds had won

the battle. We wondered what Dad would think when he saw our field of weeds, enough to provide weed seed for the entire community.

After about five years, the grasses and wildflowers slowly returned and the weeds began disappearing. With my wildflower identification book in hand, I spotted butterfly weed, two kinds of goldenrod, milkweed in profusion, and hillsides covered with brilliant blue blazing star.

In addition to the wildflowers, such native grasses as prairie June grass and little bluestem began appearing. I noticed an increase in butterflies flitting about, especially Monarchs, which are attracted to milkweed. A host of smaller butterflies of various colors appeared in the prairie, drawn by the beautiful orange butterfly weed. Honeybees and bumblebees also worked the wildflowers when they were in bloom, searching for nectar. One day I found a badger den in the prairie, a big hole in the ground with brown dirt piled up in front of it. Anthills appeared, some of them two feet high and crawling with these busy little insects. Now, some thirty years after beginning our prairie restoration, the changes continue. A year ago I spotted a big patch of needle grass growing on a side hill and on top of another hill found purple prairie clover.

Watching the transformation of these acres back to something like they were when Tom Stewart first broke the land here has been absolutely fascinating. Too often I hear from people

Goat's beard, one of nature's truly artistic creations

who want to develop a native prairie and are disappointed when it doesn't happen in a year or two. I've been observing my prairie develop for more than three decades, and the transformation continues. The joy of finding some new wildflower, grass, or butterfly is the payment I receive for my patience. The suspense of not knowing what I will discover next is part of the fun. Here I really have let nature take its course; I have planted no seeds, so whatever I find growing has gotten its beginning in some other way.

I have done little in the way of management in the prairie, except to cut rogue Scotch pine and box elder trees that appeared here and there. I had planned to do a periodic burn of my prairie, but both a DNR forester and a Federal Fish and Wildlife specialist advised against it because I have too many pines growing nearby. (Pines, of course, will burn like tinder.) So one April in the 1970s I hitched my rotary mower to the tractor and cut the dead and tangled grass. I've done this every few years since, and it has worked well, keeping volunteer trees and shrubs to a minimum and grinding up old grass and wildflower stems in preparation for a new season's growth.

ROSHARA'S PRAIRIE GRASSES

- **big bluestem** (*Andropogon gerardii*)
- **Indian grass** (*Sorghastrum nutans*)
- **little bluestem** (*Schizachyrium scoparium*)
- **needle grass** (*Stipa spartea*)
- **prairie June grass** (*Koeleria macrantha*)
- **purple love grass** (*Eragrostis spectabilis*)
- **switchgrass** (*Panicum virgatum*)

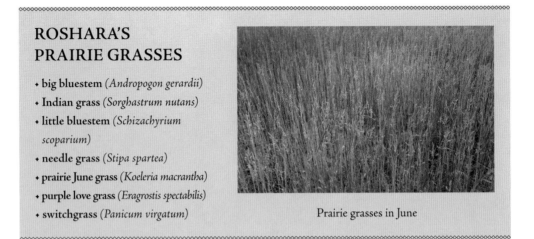

Prairie grasses in June

Starting in early spring, it seems there is something new growing or blooming in my prairie every week, right up to first frost, which usually comes in late September or early October. My laissez-faire approach to prairie restoration has been very effective, although it does take time. Nature, if given half a chance, tries to restore itself. I've found little bluestem grass and Indian grass in the prairie, and we have huge patches of purple love grass. I even have a sizable area of big bluestem grass that grows up to six feet tall on this poor land. What a treat to watch it grow each summer and produce seeds in the fall. Slowly the patch is becoming larger. Again, patience is the watchword.

I have lost my patience with the quack grass that has taken over a couple hollows in my prairie, crowding out everything else that might grow there. My next challenge is to battle this toughest of tough weedy grasses. I don't know how many hours my brothers and I spent hoeing quack grass out of the cucumber patch, the potato field, and even the hollows in the cornfields on our home farm. I suspect that long after I'm gone, country people will still cuss quack grass and debate how to get rid of it. I'm going to try once more, although ultimately I know I will fail. Quack grass has been winning for years. It will prevail.

In one of my many hikes around our newly acquired farm in 1966, I saw a carpet of purple flowers, some lighter in color, some darker, but all delicate and beautiful, on the south side of the property. This small patch of lupines (*Lupinus perennis*), about twenty or thirty feet square, grew in a little sandy, grass-free area that was exposed to full sun most of the day. It was mid-June, and the lupines were in full bloom.

On the farm where I grew up, just two miles north, I had never seen a lupine. So I knew our little patch was special. Little did I know then how special these lupines are.

In 1967 I devoted one of my newspaper columns to our lupine patch. I did some research on lupines and discovered some interesting facts. The word *lupine* (genus *Lupinus*) comes from *lupus*, the Latin name for wolf. When wolves were much more common, they were known to steal livestock from farmers. These same farmers thought that the tall, thick-growing purple-flowered plant stole nutrients from their soil, and thus they called it lupine.

While a wolf may on occasion steal a pig or a lamb from a farmer, the lupine does not steal from the soil. The opposite is true. Lupines are part of the large family of legumes (Leguminosae or Fabaceae), which also includes beans, peas, clover, and alfalfa. Legumes improve the soil thanks to nodules (little bumps) on the roots. Legumes contain bacteria that convert nitrogen in the soil into a form plants can use to grow.

Lupine

What happened next fits within the category of life's embarrassing moments. We had barely stepped into the lupine patch when Dave spotted a Karner blue. He showed it to me. I wanted to say that I had seen these butterflies all along, for years, but had thought they were the kind that resulted in cabbage worms that fed on my garden. But for once I knew to keep my mouth shut. To mistake a famous federally endangered butterfly for a lowly cabbage worm was the ultimate in biological naïveté.

Eastern tailed-blue butterfly

That fall Steve and I got out the chainsaw and clear-cut about three more acres of rogue Scotch pine from the eastern section of my prairie restoration in hopes that the lupine patch would spread and enlarge our home for the little Karner blues. Within three years, the sandy hillside where we cut the trees was covered with lupines—purple, white, deep purple, some tinged with pink. The Karner blue population expanded as well. Steve and I also discovered that the Karner blue butterfly is easily confused with other little blue butterflies that flit about our farm in early spring, especially the spring azure and the Eastern tailed-blue, both of which are similar in size and color to the Karner blue.

Karner blue butterflies are endangered or extinct in many places where they once lived. But not at Roshara. Our lupine/Karner blue restoration project is the most successful part of our entire prairie restoration. And it required little to accomplish. It took a little study, some advice and information from experts, a little tree cutting, and some patience. We have planted not one lupine plant nor collected and planted any lupine seeds. Once we removed the Scotch pines, the lupines spread on their own. The Karner blue butterflies followed.

The lupine patch has become one of our favorite places on the farm. When the lupines are in full bloom, they are a sight to behold: a sea of shimmering blue, with the occasional Karner blue butterfly adding a bit of intrigue to the mix. In many ways this part of my prairie restoration has been the most satisfying, seeing the lupines expand from a tiny plot to several acres and then discovering that we have these beautiful and very special butterflies. I sometimes think back to when Tom Stewart homesteaded this place in 1867 and wonder whether he saw lupines and Karner blues. I'm betting that he did.

WILDFLOWERS AT ROSHARA

BLUE/PURPLE
- **bird's-foot violet** (*Viola pedata*), Violet family
- **harebell** (*Campanula rotundifolia*), Bellflower family
- **leadplant** (*Amorpha canescens*), Pea family
- **Ohio spiderwort** (*Tradescantia ohiensis*), Dayflower family
- **pasqueflower** (*Pulsatilla nuttalliana*), Buttercup family
- **purple prairie clover** (*Dalea purpurea*), Pea family
- **rough blazing star** (*Liatris aspera*), Aster family
- **Russian vetch** (*Vicia villosa*), Pea family

- **smooth aster** (*Aster laevis*), several varieties
- **wild bergamot** (*Monarda fistulosa*), Mint family
- **wild lupine** (*Lupinus perennis*), Pea family

PINK
- **beardtongue** (*Penstemon grandiflorus*), Figwort family
- **columbine** (*Aquilegia canadensis*), Buttercup family
- **common milkweed** (*Asclepias syriaca*), Milkweed family

(continued on following page)

Russian vetch

- **dotted mint** (spotted bee balm) (*Monarda punctata*), Mint family
- **downy phlox** (*Phlox pilosa*), Phlox family
- **joe-pye weed** (*Eupatorium maculatum*), Aster family
- **pasture rose** (*Rosa carolina*), Rose family
- **wild geranium** (*Geranium maculatum*), Geranium family

RED AND ORANGE
- **butterfly weed** (*Asclepias tuberosa*), Milkweed family
- **cardinal flower** (*Lobelia cardinalis*), Bellflower family
- **orange hawkweed** (*Hieracium aurantiacum*), Aster family

YELLOW
- **black-eyed Susan** (*Rudbeckia hirta*), Aster family
- **butter-and-eggs** (*Linaria vulgaris*), Snapdragon family
- **common mullein** (*Verbascum thapsus*), Snapdragon family
- **early goldenrod** (*Solidago juncea*), Aster family
- **hairy puccoon** (*Lithospermum caroliniense*), Borage family

- **long-bearded hawkweed** (yellow hawkweed) (*Hieracium longipilum*), Aster family
- **meadow goat's beard** (*Tragopogon dubius*), Aster family
- **rough puccoon** (hoary puccoon) (*Lithospermum canescens*), Borage family
- **showy goldenrod** (*Solidago speciosa*), Aster family

WHITE
- **blackcap raspberry** (*Rubus occidentalis*), Rose family
- **common dewberry** (*Rubus flagellaris*), Rose family
- **daisy fleabane** (*Erigeron strigosus*), Aster family
- **false Solomon's seal** (*Smilacina racemosa*), Lily family
- **pussytoes** (*Antennaria neglecta*), Aster family
- **Solomon's seal** (*Polygonatum biflorum*), Lily family
- **white woodland aster** (*Aster divaricatus*), Aster family
- **wild strawberry** (*Fragaria virginiana*), Rose family
- **yarrow** (*Achillea millefolium*), Aster family

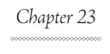

Chapter 23

Forestry

"Those are too little, Grandpa. We want those big trees to be ours."
Christian and Nicholas Apps, ages five and three

The results of thinning the pine plantation. Loggers piled the wood before hauling it to area paper mills.

My two brothers and I began planting trees at Roshara in the spring of 1966, before we had done much of anything else at the farm. We ordered one thousand red pine seedlings from the state tree nursery in Wisconsin Rapids; they arrived in mid-April. These seedling red pines, sometimes called Norway pine, were six to eight inches tall and bundled in bunches of twenty-five.

Following World War II, tree farmers in much of Waushara County had planted Christmas trees by the hundreds of thousands (the Wisconsin Christmas Tree Producers Association was formed in 1954). They planted mostly Scotch pine with the intention of shearing them (cutting off some new growth each summer). Without shearing, Scotch pine is not especially attractive, with branches spaced quite far apart. But the sheared trees grow thick and form perfect, pyramidal trees—the standard for how people used to think a Christmas tree should look.

Scotch pines grow fast, especially on sandy soils where there is little or no competition from grasses. Within eight or ten years, a Christmas tree farmer had a crop to sell. Waushara County Christmas trees were sold throughout the United States, and even today Wautoma, the county seat, prides itself on being the Christmas Tree Capital of the World.

Scotch pine seeds escaped from those Christmas tree plantations, and Scotch pines planted themselves in many places, including my farm, where they grew wild, essentially as weed trees. Other than sheared Christmas trees, Scotch pines are not particularly valuable (although I recently learned that they do have value for paper pulp). And many Scotch pines die young, at age twenty or thirty. A fungal disease attacks their root system, and it's not unusual to see them blown over by the wind, a hulk of dead and dying needles and branches.

When we bought our farm, several people asked me if we planned to plant the open fields with Christmas trees. "Make some money off those sandy acres," a neighbor said. I replied that we wanted to leave the old fields open and didn't want acres of Christmas trees. It was a wise decision. In the early 2000s the Christmas tree market, especially the demand for sheared Scotch pine, started to decline. Those who still buy live trees seem to prefer the more elegant Fraser fir, which is a slow grower, but a beautiful tree.

Red pines grow rapidly, are long-lived and beautiful, and when mature have considerable economic value. The paper mills like them; so do the log cabin sawmills. Mature trees are also suitable for sawed lumber.

Seedlings are planted in mid- to late April, when the frost is out of the ground, the soil moisture is high, and the seedlings are still dormant. The sooner after receiving the nursery stock, the better it is to plant them. We planted our first thousand red pines in four rows around our

Balsam fir seedling

farm boundaries. Every bit of our tree planting project was hard work. We hitched a one-bottom walking plow to Dad's Farmall H tractor, and with my brother Donald's and Dad's help I plowed four furrows along the front boundary of the farm and four more along the south boundary. I walked slowly behind the plow, holding the handles and recalling what it had been like when I used this same plow, but with a team of horses providing the power.

Planting the trees in furrows would give the little red pines an early advantage against grass competition. The open furrows would also capture and retain moisture when it rained. With the furrows made, we worked in two-person teams, Ruth and me, my Dad and Donald (the kids, still tykes at the time, also "helped"). One person walked backward, making a slit in the bottom of the furrow with a shovel. The second person, carrying fifty or so trees in a bucket of water, selected a tree and stuck it in the slit, making sure all the little roots were in the hole. The first person pushed the slit shut with his foot, removing all the air and forcing the soft, sandy soil around the tree's roots; then he or she backed up six feet and made another slit. The process continued. We planted rows of trees about eight feet apart, little tree after little

Heavy rains have cut deep gullies at several places on the farm.

PART IV

A Sense of Place

The pond provides a place for solitude.

opposites. But not for me. Connecting and being disconnected are part of the same phenomenon. I need both, regularly and in near equal amounts. It is not difficult to find opportunities to be with others—indeed, the invitations to do so come regularly. It is more difficult to find the opportunity to be alone these days, especially in the face of those who do not subscribe to its importance and who see those who seek it as antisocial and strange. And so I travel to Roshara, often alone for several days, in search of solitude.

I am stimulated by others. New ideas fly around the room during a good discussion. I especially appreciated my graduate students at the University of Wisconsin, since our earliest days at Roshara. They bombarded me with fresh ideas, new ways of connecting old thoughts, questions I couldn't answer, perspectives I'd never considered. But after hours of this rich stimulation, I needed to escape, to find a place alone where I could make sense of all that I was taking in—these raw and unexamined ideas and perspectives. So I sought the solitude of my land. I would sit on a hill at the back of the farm and try and make sense out of all that my mind had received.

As I told my students, I am constantly searching for my own truth, my own take on matters, my perspective, my way of understanding the world. I resist the blank acceptance of others' truths as my own, no matter how powerful their reputations, how careful their arguments, or how passionate their pleas. But I listen carefully to other people's positions, whether they are students or learned scholars (whatever that means). I force myself to consider the perspectives of those who appear to have different views from what I value and believe. My stance is that I cannot know what I believe about something unless I know what I *don't* believe, unless I know the counterargument to my position. Thus, I go looking for unusual perspectives, arguments that on the surface anger or agitate me, beliefs that astound and surprise me. It is the old, tired perspectives, spoken in rote and repeated again and again, that tire me and turn me away, turn me off.

Solitude allows you to discover the you that you may not know exists. It is a way to see bigger pictures and larger connections. In solitude we can think through problems slowly and deliberately, searching for and considering multiple perspectives and alternative solutions.

My farm is a place for solitude, where I can sit on the edge of my prairie at sunset on a warm summer evening with a cool southwest breeze washing over me, or walk the trail through the woods on a cool day in autumn when the aspen are deep yellow and the maples bright red. Snowshoe to the pond on a winter day when fresh snow gathers on my coat and

Winter is a quiet, restful time at the farm.

I can see but a few feet in front of me because the snow is falling so fast. Watch raindrops strike the smooth surface of the pond, each little whirlpool becoming ever larger and disappearing, only to be replaced again and again by other raindrops.

Like me, Ruth craves solitude. Her favorite place is on top of the hill, near the white pine windbreak, where she can see across the expanse of our prairie. There a soft breeze rustles the pine needles, the horizon is far in the distance, and the subtle smells of the outdoors surround her. A bench is tucked under a pine tree—Ruth's bench. This is her spot for solitude.

Over the years, I have introduced my children and grandchildren to solitude and its values—not an easy thing to teach, if indeed it can be taught at all. Solitude is personal, to be discovered, and Roshara is a place to do it.

Chapter 27

◇◇◇◇◇◇◇◇◇◇◇◇◇◇◇◇◇◇

Roshara Sounds

"The silence was beyond the ordinary sounds of nature; it dealt with distance, timelessness, and a perception, a sense of being engulfed by something greater where minor sounds were only a part, a hush embedded in our consciousness."

Sigurd Olson

A pair of sandhill cranes nests at the pond each year. Their prehistoric call is distinctive.

Snow-covered
trees hang low over
a farm trail.

Some people love the noise of the city, say it makes them feel alive, gives them a sense of oneness with a vibrant place. But not this country boy. I seek the quiet of the country. Many of my city friends have grown up in the city, love it, respect it, and could not live anywhere else. Most of them are uneasy when there are moments of utter quiet, when there is a break in a radio program or when the TV screen goes blank for a few seconds. They'll switch stations, not content to have a few moments of silence within the blare of continuous programming.

The country is not entirely a quiet place. But there are moments when there is little or no sound. Of course, the ideal country place has no background traffic noise, but those places are becoming more difficult to find as highways and automobiles are sneaking into the far corners of the countryside, invading the quiet and destroying remoteness.

The sounds of the country change with the seasons, especially here in the Midwest, where seasonal change is often dramatic. The sounds of winter are the northwest wind sifting across my prairie, picking up wisps of snow and dropping it again in intricate patterns, rills and ridges, swirls and squiggles. On a cold night in January, the sound of winter is the wind tearing at the cabin, trying to seep in around the windows and doors, challenging my woodstoves, and making a most mournful sound in the process.

Winter sounds can also be the most subtle. On a still day in November, when the temperature is just below freezing and the first heavy snow of the season arrives, the snowflakes, some of them huge, fall ever so lightly on naked tree limbs and dead prairie grass.

An unexpected sound is that of tree fibers exploding on below-zero days. I remember walking in our oak woods one quiet January morning, when the temperature was ten below zero. The only sound was the occasional crow calling in the distance, until I heard what I was sure was a rifle shot. I learned later from my father that it was tree fibers loudly protesting the cold. The sound happens infrequently enough to surprise the cold-weather walker in the woods each time he or she hears it.

The most mysterious of winter sounds might be the northwest wind shaking the dead leaves of the black oaks that still hang on the branches. Some have called this sound a death rattle—and in a way it is. The oak leaves hang on until spring and then finally fall off to make way for new growth and the summer sound of warm breezes moving through green leaves.

Country people wait for the most joyous sound of all, especially if the winter has been long and cold. It comes usually in March, when the wind swings around to the south and the temperature creeps above freezing for a few days. Meltwater begins dripping from the cabin roof and running in rivulets down the trail leading to the white pine woods. It is a sound of celebration. A time for stopping work and listening to the first hints of spring. A time to begin looking forward with anticipation instead of marking time as winter days seem to go on forever.

Soon the sounds of spring fill the air at Roshara, with the first robin song, sometimes when snow piles still line the driveway. The call of Canada geese rings out, the birds flying in formation from their wintering grounds in southern Illinois to the northern reaches of Canada. On an early spring morning it is not uncommon to hear male turkeys gobbling deep in the woods west of our pond. A ruffed grouse's drumming, a crow cawing, or an owl hooting will set them off, prompting a gobbler to let loose with a loud, "gobble, gobble, gobble." And not to be forgotten, sandhill cranes that nest at the pond sound that primitive, rattling call.

When the spring peepers begin their evening chant, I know for sure spring is here. These tiny frogs who live near the pond sing in unison—hundreds of them, perhaps thousands. On a warm, still night their sound engulfs the valley around the pond.

Slowly, imperceptibly, the sounds of summer emerge: the rumble of distant thunder, the deep "jug of rum, more rum" call of the bullfrogs at the pond, the loud snort of a deer when she first discovers me, the dry sound of an August wind moving over the parched prairie, the nervous quivering of aspen leaves, the chatting of a wren outside our bedroom window, and, on occasional hot nights, the sawing of cicadas.

And then the crickets take over the night, and I know it's fall. Occasionally we hear a coyote yapping or an owl calling. And in the morning there is the crunching sound when I walk on frost-covered grass to fetch an armload of wood from the woodshed and I catch the sound of a high-flying V of Canada geese. In the cabin I soon hear the snap and pop of pine kindling wood as the fire in the woodstove comes to life once more.

At the edge of the prairie, a solitary bluebird house awaits the arrival of its first spring occupant.

Chapter 28

◇◇◇◇◇◇◇◇◇◇◇◇◇◇◇◇◇◇

Living on the Land

"When one tugs at a single thing in nature, he finds it attached to the rest of the world."
JOHN MUIR

When my father first bought this old farm in 1964, his neighbors wondered why he was buying more land, and at his age (he was sixty-four at the time). He already owned 160 acres, which he had farmed almost his entire life. Why buy a farm that in the minds of most people, especially farmers, was right close to worthless property? The buildings were falling down; the house had burned. The land was sandy, hilly, and in some places stony. Most of its fields hadn't raised a decent crop for years, if ever. The previous owner had rented out a couple of less hilly fields to a neighbor for corn. But unless it rained every week during the summer—which seldom happened—the corn was doomed to a low yield at best and dried-up plants at worst.

"Don't really know why I bought the place," Dad said to his neighbors, who shook their heads, wondering if Dad had slipped a cog or two as he'd gotten older. But Dad knew what he was doing; he just didn't think his neighbors would understand if he tried to explain it. Besides being a farmer, Dad was keenly interested in wildlife, trees, wildflowers, and birds. He enjoyed sunrises and sunsets, snowstorms and thunder, first snow and the coming of spring. He liked the smell of freshly turned soil and dead grass in August, the sounds of the country night—whip-poor-wills, hoot owls, and crickets. And he loved the seasonal changes, looking forward to each with great anticipation—spring's plowing and planting, summer's harvests, fall's leaves turning color, and winter's slowing down and opportunities to go ice fishing.

Dad was captivated by the land and its multiple meanings and uses. Although I never heard him say it, land was important to him, and his relationship to it was deep and enduring.

The United States does not have an especially good record of how its residents have treated the land. Upon meeting the Native Americans who had fished, hunted, and cultivated the country for thousands of years, the first settlers couldn't understand the Native American philosophy expressed in such phrases as, "The land is sacred," "We and the land are one," "Mother Earth."

The first thing white settlers wanted was to own land. Some early pioneers in central Wisconsin bought newly surveyed land for as little as $1.25 an acre and set out to eke out a living for their families by growing a few crops and raising a few hogs and a couple cows. They were subsistence farmers. For these early settlers, cheap land meant a chance to improve their lives. Many of these early landowners quickly learned that never-before-plowed land would grow spectacular crops of wheat. Soon this former Indian country had been transformed into thousands of acres of wheat. The land view had moved from the sacred to the mundane—from something to be revered to a commercial opportunity.

By the late 1860s wheat growing dwindled, yields plummeted, insects and disease took their toll, and farmers slowly shifted from wheat to dairy farming. Land use changed again. Farmers had learned to rotate their crops: oats, hay crops, pasture, and corn. Cow manure spread back on the fields provided fertilizer, and wheat-worn fields slowly improved.

By the 1950s, with mechanization including milking machines, tractors, field combines, and forage harvesters, dairy farms began increasing in size, as did dairy herds. A farm of 160 acres was no longer large enough to support sufficient cows to be competitive. So farms got bigger, dairy herds grew larger, and farmers with smaller acreages or those with poorer soils were forced to sell.

On the poorer, hillier farms of central Wisconsin, yet another shift in land use unfolded. Former small dairy farms became private hunting preserves, the land essentially allowed to go back to trees. Other little farms met a different fate: they were chopped up into smaller pieces and sold for home building. At the 160-acre farm where I grew up, a home now stands on each of four twenty-acre fields—some modest manufactured homes, one a huge trophy house. Forty acres are devoted to Christmas tree growing. On the remaining forty stand the original homestead buildings—house, barn, granary, pump house—an original oak woodlot, and another new home on a few acres.

I believe it is important that some parcels of land remain whole. Many wild creatures, including owls, bears, pileated woodpeckers, and even songbirds such as scarlet tanagers, prefer larger areas to live, away from close proximity with humans. For those of us who seek out areas of quiet, larger tracts of land offer sound buffers from traffic noise. And from an aesthetic perspective, nothing is more pleasing to me than looking out over a vast tract of land to the north of my farm. Roshara sits within an area of about seven hundred acres of mostly wooded land—four little lakes and my prairie are the exceptions—that is together in one piece as it has always been, with no road cutting through it. Several people own these acres, but for a variety of reasons they have chosen to leave them as they have always been. Many of these acres have never been farmed, in particular those that surround the lakes. In 2001, as he semiretired, my brother Donald and his wife, Marcie, built a permanent home on his portion of the farm, just to the south of our property. My father would have been pleased to have a permanent resident on the farm, looking out for it as well as enjoying it.

My personal views about land, developed from my growing-up years on a farm and from my forty-plus years caring for Roshara, include a strong belief that land is something to cherish and revere, to pass on to those who follow in better condition than when it was acquired. Our farm is a source of fresh vegetables for eating, trails for hiking, paths for skiing and snowshoeing, hills for sunset watching, fields for running, wildflowers to appreciate, and birds and animals to study. It is a storehouse of history and stories.

My land is also a guide and a listener. When I face some crisis in my life—the loss of a loved one, a professional disappointment, a health challenge—I sit on a hill surrounded by sky and acres of trees and grass. This helps me heal.

My farm is always changing, but forever the same. I know a good deal about this old place, but there remains much more to learn. I try to follow what others have taught me: to listen, watch, experience, study, dig into history, look for old barbwire, search out a gully, watch a hawk soar on a cloudless day—and never forget to take care of the land.

Appendix

SOURCES AND TIPS FOR RESEARCHING LAND AND ANCESTORS

Every piece of land has a story to tell. The more I learned about my farm, the more stories emerged—and the more digging I wanted to do. I had learned something about the farm from the neighbors who had passed on stories from generation to generation as a part of the oral history of the place: stories of Indians who camped at our pond and visited the homestead bartering maple sugar for salt; tales about the farming strategies of the Coombes family, who owned our farm before we did. (It seemed all the neighbors had stories about Weston Coombes and his mother, Ina, and their trips around the area with horse and buggy during the years when everyone else drove a car.)

After we bought the place, neighbors were quick to point out that it "wasn't much of a farm." They were referring to the hilly and rocky land and the sandy soil. The more I heard, the more questions I had. Why was the region so sandy, hilly, and studded with stones? And what about the Indians who had camped on the pond—who were they, why were they traveling across what later became our land? Could I learn more about the Coombes family, something of their background and their history? It seemed the more I learned about the place, the more remained to be discovered. Over the past forty years I've learned a considerable amount about the farm, but more stories lurk on these acres.

For those who want to learn more about a particular piece of land, here are a few tips. Most of the digging for information can be a bit tedious, with a fair share of dead ends and disappointment, but, oh, what joy it is to uncover a kernel of new knowledge. Perhaps the most fruitful bit of information I uncovered in my search was first landowner Tom Stewart's Civil War records. With those records, I now had a copy of his marriage license, a list of his children, his medical records—I learned more about Tom Stewart than about almost anyone I know.

Some of the best places to look for information are city and town halls, county courthouses, local historical societies, local libraries, cemeteries, and knowledgeable people in the community. The Wisconsin Historical Society in Madison is a wonderful source of all kinds of information,

The pond reflects the vivid fall colors of maples and aspen.

Notes

CHAPTER 3

1. Lawrence Martin, *The Physical Geography of Wisconsin* (Madison: University of Wisconsin Press, 1965), 235–270.

2. A. R. Whitson, W. J. Geib, G. Conroy, A. K. Kuhlman, and J. W. Nelson, *Soil Survey of Waushara County* (Madison: Wisconsin Geological and Natural History Survey, 1913).

3. Augustine J. Otter, Fred J. Simeth, and Duane T. Simonson, *Soil Survey of Waushara Country, Wisconsin* (Madison: USDA Soil Conservation Service and College of Agricultural and Life Sciences, University of Wisconsin–Madison, 1989).

4. Ibid., 34.

5. Ibid., 20.

6. A. R. Whitson, W. J. Geib, G. Conroy, A. K. Kuhlman, and J. W. Nelson. *Soil Survey of Waushara County* (Madison: Wisconsin Geological and Natural History Survey, 1913).

7. United States Department of Agriculture, National Agricultural Statistics Service, Wisconsin-Waushara County, 2006.

8. John T. Curtis, *The Vegetation of Wisconsin* (Madison: University of Wisconsin Press, 1959, 1971), 15–24.

9. Lawrence Martin, *The Physical Geography of Wisconsin* (Madison: University of Wisconsin Press, 1965), 254–255.

CHAPTER 4

1. "Exterior Field Notes T21N R9E R10E," May 9, 1851, *Wisconsin Public Land Survey Records: Original Field Notes and Plat Maps*.

2. Ibid., 53.

3. "Interior Field Notes," October 2, 1851, *Wisconsin Public Land Survey Records: Original Field Notes and Plat Maps*, 300.

4. Ibid., 345.

5. Ibid.

6. Felix Keesing, *The Menomini Indians of Wisconsin: A Study of Three Centuries of Cultural Contact and Change* (Madison: University of Wisconsin Press, 1987), 140–147.

7. Ibid., 139.

8. Ibid., 141.

9. Ibid., 142.

10. *Wisconsin Public Land Survey Records: Original Field Notes and Plat Maps*.

11. "Interior Field Notes," October 2, 1851, *Wisconsin Public Land Survey Records: Original Field Notes and Plat Maps*, 319.

12. Bureau of Land Management, *Wisconsin Land Patents Database: Waushara County*, Washington, DC: National Archives.

13. Ibid.

CHAPTER 5

1. John M. Woodward, unpublished manuscript, c. 1925, Wild Rose Historical Society, Wild Rose, WI.

2. Ibid.

3. Ibid.

CHAPTER 6

1. Roster Wisconsin Volunteers, 35th Infantry, Company 5, 566.

2. William Striedy, Affidavit to Origin of Disability, May June, 1897, U.S. National Archives and Records Administration, Full Pension File, Thomas Stewart.

3. James Gustins, Affidavit for Commissioned Officer or Comrade, no date, U.S. National Archives and Records Administration, Full Pension File, Thomas Stewart.

4. War Department, Adjutant General's Office, October 30, 1882, U.S. National Archives and Records Administration, Full Pension File, Thomas Stewart.

5. Abstract of Title, Lands in Section 33-20-10. Waushara Abstract Corporation, Wautoma, WI. Abstract Number 215, 1.

6. Richard Current, *The History of Wisconsin.* Vol. II, *The Civil War Era 1848–1873* (Madison: State Historical Society of Wisconsin, 1976), 94.

7. Ibid., 92.

8. Certificate of Marriage, Tom Stewart and Maria Jenks, August 28, 1869, Register of Deeds, Waushara County, Wautoma, WI.

9. Bureau of Land Management, *Wisconsin Land Patents Database: Waushara County*, Washington, DC: National Archives.

10. State of Wisconsin Census, Town of Rose, Waushara County, June 1875.

11. The *Waushara Argus* (Wautoma, WI), June 9, 1875.

12. John M. Woodward, unpublished manuscript, c. 1925, Wild Rose Historical Society, Wild Rose, WI.

13. "Wild Rose History, Stories by Members," unpublished manuscript, no date, Patterson Memorial Library, Wild Rose, WI.

14. Cemetery Records, Mt. Pleasant Cemetery (Standalone Cemetery), Waushara County, WI.

CHAPTER 7

1. Waushara Abstract Corporation, Wautoma, WI, Abstract of Title, Lands in Section 33-20-10, Abstract Number 215, 1–15.

2. *Portrait and Biographical Album of Green Lake, Marquette and Waushara Counties, Wisconsin* (Chicago: Acme Publishing Company, 1890).

3. Minutes of Village Board, Wild Rose, WI, C. A. Smart, President, April 25, 1904.

4. Notice, *Wild Rose Times* (Wild Rose, WI), March 19, 1905.

5. Waushara Abstract Corporation, Wautoma, WI, Abstract of Title, Lands in Section 33-20-10, Abstract Number 215, 1–15.

6. Minutes of Village Board, Wild Rose, WI, August 1, 1908.

7. *Wild Rose Times* (Wild Rose, WI), February 15, 1912.

8. *Atlas and Farmers' Directory, Rose Township* (St. Paul, MN: The Farmer, circa 1913), 11.

9. Ibid.

10. Ibid.

CHAPTER 15

1. Virgil J. Vogel. *Indian Names on Wisconsin's Map* (Madison: University of Wisconsin Press, 1991), 64.

CHAPTER 16

1. Rob Nurre, personal correspondence, September 5, 2006.

CHAPTER 18

1. Diana Wells, *100 Flowers and How They Got Their Names* (Chapel Hill, NC: Algonquin Books, 1997), 62–63.

2. Ibid., 121–122.

Index

Jerry Apps is professor emeritus at the University of Wisconsin–Madison and the author of many books on rural history and country life, including *The Quiet Season: Remembering Country Winters, Limping through Life: A Farm Boy's Polio Memoir, Barns of Wisconsin, Horse-Drawn Days: A Century of Farming with Horses,* and *Ringlingville USA.* Among his many awards are the Council for Wisconsin Writers' Major Achievement Award, the Wisconsin Library Association's Notable Wisconsin Author Award, and the Distinguished

Service Award from the University of Wisconsin College of Agricultural and Life Sciences. He was inducted as a Fellow to the Wisconsin Academy of Sciences, Arts and Letters in 2012 and starred in the Wisconsin Public Television programs *A Farm Story with Jerry Apps* and *A Farm Winter with Jerry Apps.*

Jerry was born and raised on a small farm in Waushara County, Wisconsin, about two miles from the land that is the subject of *Old Farm.* He and his family have owned Roshara since 1966.

Steve Apps is an award-winning photojournalist with twenty-three years in the newspaper industry. As a *Wisconsin State Journal* staff photographer he has covered a wide range of assignments including the Green Bay Packers and University of Wisconsin–Madison sports. In 2008 he received the Pro Football Hall of Fame's prestigious Dave Boss Award of Excellence; his photo "First Down" was selected as Photograph of the Year for the 2007 season.

AUTHOR PHOTOS BY STEVE APPS